Rachel Walter Shoemaker

Classic Dialogues and Dramas

Rachel Walter Shoemaker

Classic Dialogues and Dramas

ISBN/EAN: 9783337340889

Printed in Europe, USA, Canada, Australia, Japan

Cover: Foto ©Thomas Meinert / pixelio.de

More available books at **www.hansebooks.com**

SHOEMAKER'S
Best Selections

FOR

READINGS AND RECITATIONS

Numbers 1 to 28 Now Issued

Paper Binding, each number,   -   -   30 cents

Cloth   ''   ''   ''   -   -   -   50   ''

This series was formerly called "The Elocutionist's Annual," the first 17 numbers being published under that title. The change in name is made because it is believed a more appropriate title is thus secured.

Teachers, Readers, Students, and all persons who have occasion to use books of this kind, concede this to be the best series of speakers published. The different numbers are compiled by leading elocutionists of the country, who have exceptional facilities for securing selections, and whose judgment as to their merits is invaluable. No trouble or expense is spared to obtain the very best readings and recitations, and much material is used by special arrangement with other publishers, thus securing the best selections from such American authors as Longfellow, Holmes, Whittier, Lowell, Emerson, Alice and Phœbe Cary, Mrs. Stowe, and many others. The foremost English authors are also represented, as well as the leading French and German writers.

Sold by all Booksellers and Newsdealers, or mailed upon receipt of price.

THE PENN PUBLISHING CO.
1020 Arch Street

CLASSIC

DIALOGUES

AND

DRAMAS

COMPILED BY

MRS. J. W. SHOEMAKER

Philadelphia
The Penn Publishing Company
1895

CONTENTS.

CLASSIC
DIALOGUES AND DRAMAS.

SCENE FROM DAMON AND PYTHIAS.
Adapted.

A scaffold, with steps ascending to it.—In the back of the stage the gates of a prison.—Executioner with an Axe, and Guards discovered.

Enter DAMOCLES *and* PROCLES.

Proc.—It is a marvelous phantasy, thou speakest of
In Dionysius.

Dam.—Yes, his mind is made
Of strange materials, that are almost cast
In contrariety to one another.
The school and camp, in his ambition, make
A strange division: "with the trumpet's call
He blends the languor of the poet's lyre!
The fierce, intrepid captain of the field
Hath often, on the great Athenian stage,
Coped with the mightiest monarchs of the Muse;
And, in mine apprehension, he doth prize
The applauses of that polished populace,
More than the rising shout of victory.

Proc.—"And, over all, that science, which doth hold,
Touching the soul and its affections,
5

Its high discoursing, hath attracted him."
It is his creed, that, in this flesh of ours,
Self ever entertains predominance;
And, to all friendship, he hath ever been
A persevering infidel.   For this,
Belike, he tries a strange experiment.
What sayest thou?   Will Damon come again?
 Dam.—"Our love of life is in the very instinct
Of mere material action, when we do
Even so slight a thing, as wink an eye
Against the wind.   Place me a soulless dog
Upon the bare edge of a height, and he
Shall shudder and shrink back, though none have proved
To his capacity that the fall were dangerous."
I hold the thing impossible.
 Proc.—He'll not!
 Dam.—What, when he feels his pent-up soul abroad,
His limbs unfettered, "and the mountain-breeze
Of liberty all around him, and his life
Or death upon his own free choice dependent?"
'Tis visionary!
 Proc.—But is there no hope
Of Dionysius' mercy?
 Dam.—He'll not give
A second's hundredth part to take a chance in.
"His indignation swells at such a rashness,
That, in its fling of proud philosophy,
Can make him feel so much out-soared and humbled."
What a vast multitude upon the hills
Stretch their long blackening outline in the round
Of the blue heavens!
 Proc.—They wait the great event.
"Mute expectation spreads its anxious hush

O'er the wide city, that as silent stands
As its reflection in the quiet sea."
Behold, upon the roof what thousands gaze
Toward the distant road that leads to Syracuse.
An hour ago a noise was heard afar,
Like to the pulses of the restless surge;
But as the time approaches, all grows still
As the wide dead of midnight!

[*The gates of the prison are flung open, and* PYTHIAS *is
discovered. He advances to the scaffold.*
    [*To the Executioner.*] There is no pang in thy
deep wedge of steel.
Nay, sir, you may spare
Yourself the pains to fit me for the block.—
Damon, I do forgive thee!—I but ask
Some tears unto my ashes!
    [*A distant shout is heard.—Pythias leaps upon the
scaffold.*
By the gods
A horse and horseman!—Far upon the hill,
They wave their hats, and he returns it—yet
I know him not—his horse is at the stretch! [*A shout.*
Why should they shout as he comes on? It is—
No!—that was too unlike—but there, now—there!·
Oh, life, I scarcely dare to wish for thee;
And yet—that jutting rock has hid him from me—
No!—let it not be Damon!—he has a wife
And child!—gods!—keep him back!—   [*Shouts.*
    Damon.—[*Without.*] Where is he!

DAMON *rushes in, and stands for a moment looking round.*
Ha!
He is alive! untouched! Ha! ha! ha!

[*Falls with an hysterical laugh upon the stage.*—
Three loud shouts without.

Pyth.—The gods do know I could have died for him!
And yet I dared to doubt!—I dared to breathe
The half-uttered blasphemy!   [*Damon is raised up.*
He faints!—How thick
This wreath of burning moisture on his brow!
His face is black with toil, his swelling bulk
Heaves with swift pantings.   Damon, my dear friend!
    Damon.—Where am I?   Have I fallen from my horse,
That I am stunned, and on my head I feel
A weight of thickening blood!—What has befallen me!
The horrible confusion of a dream
Is yet upon my sight.—For mercy's sake,
Stay me not back—he is about to die!
Pythias, my friend!   Unloose me, villains, or
You'll find the might of madness in mine arm!
[*Sees Pythias.*]   Speak to me, let me hear thy voice!
    Pyth.—My friend!
    Damon.—It pierced my brain, and rushed into my
        heart!
There's lightning in it!—That's the scaffold—there
The block—the axe—the executioner!
And here he lives!—I have him in my soul!
[*Embraces Pythias.*]   Ha! ha! ha!
    Pyth.—Damon!
    Damon.—Ha! ha!
I can but laugh!—I cannot speak to thee!
I can but play the maniac, and laugh!
Thy hand!—Oh, let me grasp thy manly hand!—
It is an honest one, and so is mine!
They are fit to clasp each other!   Ha! ha! ha!

Pyth.—Would that my death could have preserved
  thee!

Damon—Pythias,
Even in the very crisis to have come,—
To have hit the very forehead of old time!
By heavens! had I arrived an hour before,
I should not feel this agony of joy—
This triumph over Dionysius!
Ha! ha!—But did'st thou doubt me? Come, thou did'st—
Own it, and I'll forgive thee.

  Pyth.—For a moment.

  Damon.—Oh, that false slave!—Pythias, he slew my
    horse,
In the base thought to save me! I would have killed
    him,
And to a precipice was dragging him,
When, from the very brink of the abyss,
I did behold a traveler afar,
Bestriding a good steed—I rushed upon him,
Choking with desperation, and yet loud
In shrieking anguish, I commanded him
Down from his saddle: he denied me—but
Would I then be denied? as hungry tigers
Clutch their poor prey, I sprang upon his throat:
Thus, thus, I had him, Pythias! Come, your horse,
Your horse, your horse, I cried. Ha! ha! ha!

  Dion.—[*Advancing and speaking in a loud tone.*]
    Damon!

  Damon.—[*Jumping on the scaffold.*] I am here upon
    the scaffold! look at me:
I am standing on my throne; as proud a one
As yon illumined mountain, where the sun
Makes his last stand; let him look on me too;

He never did behold a spectacle
More full of natural glory.   Death is—[*Shouts.*]   Ha!
All Syracuse starts up upon her hills,
And lifts her hundred thousand hands.   [*Shouts.*]   She
 shouts,   [*Shouts.*
Hark, how she shouts!   [*Shouts.*]   O Dionysius!
When wert thou in thy life hailed with a peal
Of hearts and hands like that one?   Shout again!
             [*Shouts.*

Again! [*Shouts*] until the mountains echo you,
And the great sea joins in that mighty voice,
And old Euceladus, the Son of Earth,
Stirs in his mighty caverns.   [*Three shouts.*]   Tell me,
 slaves,
Where is your tyrant?   Let me see him now;
Why stands he hence aloof?   Where is your master?
What is become of Dionysius?
I would behold, and laugh at him!
  [*Dionysius advances between Damon and Pythias—
  Damon being on the scaffold—and throws off his
  disguise.*
 Dion.—Behold me.
 Damon and Pyth.—How?
 Dion.—Stay your admiration for awhile,
Till I have spoken my commandment here.
Go, Damocles, and bid a herald cry
Wide through the city, from the eastern gate
Unto the most remote extremity,
That Dionysius, tyrant as he is,
Gives back his life to Damon.   [*Exit Damocles.*
 Pyth.—How, Dionysius?
Speak that again!
 Dion.—I pardon him.

Pyth.—O gods!
You give his life to Damon?
Dion.—Life and freedom!
  [*Shouts, drums.—Damon staggers from the scaffold
  into the arms of Pythias.*
                    CURTAIN FALLS.
                                        JOHN BANIM.

———•———

SPEECHES OF ZENOBIA AND HER COUNCIL IN REFERENCE TO THE ANTICIPATED WAR WITH ROME.

Adapted.

———

CHARACTERS.—Zenobia, Queen of Palmyra; Gracchus, a Roman and the Queen's chief adviser and head of the Senate; Longinus, a Greek philosopher and a prominent member of the Senate; Otho, a Palmyrean nobleman and a Senator; Zabdas, an Egyptian and General-in-chief of the Queen's army; also present, the Princess Julia; Fausta, daughter of Gracchus, and Lucius Piso, a Roman nobleman; two young and beautiful female slaves in attendance, one with cushion for foot-rest, the other with large fan of peacock feathers, seated at the feet of the Queen, to do her service.

Scenery and costume will add greatly to the rendition of this scene, and if used, should be in adaptation to time, character, rank, and nationality.

Disposition of Characters.—Zenobia seated upon her throne, surrounded by her friends, some sitting, others standing without order about her.

Queen.—Good friends, I believe one thought fills every mind present here. Is it not better that we give it utterance? I need the sympathy and the counsel of those who love me. But I ask not only for the opinions of those who agree with me, but as sincerely for those of such as may differ from me. You know me well in this, that I refuse not to hearken to reasons, the strongest that can be devised, although they oppose my own settled judgment. Let us freely open our minds each to the other, and let no one fear to offend me but by withholding his full and free opinion.

Gracchus.—We, who know our Queen so well, hardly need these assurances. Were I as bitterly opposed to the measures proposed as I am decidedly in favor of them, I should none the less fearlessly and frankly declare the reasons of my dissent. I am sure that every one here experiences the freedom you enjoin. But who will need to use it? For are we not of one mind? I see, indeed, one or two who oppose the general sentiment. But for the rest, one spirit animates all, and, what is more, to the farthest limits of the kingdom am I persuaded the same spirit spreads, and possesses and fills every soul. The attempt of Aurelian to control us in our affairs, to dictate to us concerning the limits of our empire, so far removed, is felt to be a wanton freak of despotic power, which, if it be not withstood in its first encroachment, may proceed to other acts less tolerable still, and which may leave us scarcely our name as a distinct people—and that covered with shame. Although a Roman by descent, I advocate not Roman intolerance. I can see and denounce injustice in Aurelian as well as in another. Palmyra is my country and Zenobia my Queen, and when I seek not their honor, may my own fall blasted and ruined. I stand ready to pledge for them in this emergency, what every other man of Palmyra holds it his privilege to offer, my property and my life, and if I have any possession dearer than these, I am ready to bring and lay it upon the same altar.

Longinus.—The gods weave the texture of our souls, not ourselves; and the web is too intensely wove and drenched in too deep a dye for us to undo or greatly change. The eagle cannot be tamed down to the softness of a dove, and no art of the husbandman can send to the gnarled and knotted oak the juices that shall smooth and melt its stiffness into the yielding pliancy of the willow. I wage no war with the work of the gods. Besides, the demands of Rome have now grown to such a size that they swallow up our very existence as a free and sovereign State. They leave us but this single city and province out of an empire that now stretches from the Nile to the Bosphorus—an empire obtained by what cost of blood and treasure I need not say, any more than by what consummate skill in that art which boasts the loftiest minds of all ages. Palmyra not only owes a duty to herself in this matter, but to the whole East, and even to the world. For what part of the civilized world has not been trampled into dust by the despotism of almighty Rome? It is needful to the well-being of nations that some power shall boldly stand forth and check an insolence that suffers no city nor kingdom to rest in peace. No single people ought to obtain universal empire. A powerful nation is the more observant of the eternal principles of honor and justice for being watched by another, its equal. Individual character needs such supervision, and national as much. Palmyra is now an imposing object in the eye of the whole world. It is the second power. All I wish is, that for the sake of the world's peace it shall retain this position. I deprecate conquest. However another may aspire to victory over Aurelian, to new additions from the Roman territory, I have no such aspirations. On the other hand, I shall deplore any success beyond the maintenance of a just and honorable independence. This is our right by inheritance, and as much also by conquest, and for this I am ready, with the noble Gracchus, to offer to my sovereign my properties, my powers, and my life. If my poor life can prolong by a single year the reign of one who, with virtues so eminent and a genius so vast, fills the throne of this fair kingdom, I would lay it at her feet with joy, and think it a service well done for our own and the world's happiness.

Otho.—My opinions are well known, and it may be needless that I should again, and especially here, declare them, seeing that they will jar so rudely with those entertained by you, my friends around me.. But sure I am, that no one has advocated the cause and the sentiments which Zenobia cherishes so fondly with a truer, deeper affection for her, with a sincerer love of her glory, than I rise to oppose them with—

Queen (interrupting).—We know it! we know it! Otho.

Otho.—Thanks, noble Queen, for the fresh assurance of it. It is because I love, that I resist you. It is because I glory in your reign, in your renown, in your virtues, that I oppose an enterprise that I see with a prophet's vision will tarnish them all. Were I your enemy, I could not do better than to repeat the arguments that have just fallen from the lips of the head of our coun‐ cils, set off with every trick of eloquence that would send them with a yet more resistless power into the minds, not only of those who are assembled here, but of those, your subjects, wherever over these large domin‐ ions they are scattered. To press this war is to under‐ mine the foundations of the fairest kingdom the sun shines upon, and unseat the most beloved ruler that ever swayed a sceptre over the hearts of a devoted people. It can have no other issue. And this is not, O noble Queen! to throw discredit upon former achievements, or to express a doubt of powers which have received the homage of the world; it is only with open eyes to acknowledge what all but the blind must see and confess, the overwhelming superiority in power of every kind of the other party.   We may gain a single victory —to that genius and courage are equal, and we possess them in more than even Roman measure—but that very victory may be our undoing, or but embitter the temper of the enemy, call forth a new display of unexhausted and unexhaustible resources, while our very good success itself will have nearly annihilated our armies.   And what can happen then but ruin, absolute and complete ? Roman magnanimity may spare our city and our name.   But it is more likely that Roman vengeance may blot them both out from the map of the world, and leave us nought but the fame of our Queen and the crumbling ruins of this once flourishing city by which to be remembered by posterity.   These are not the counsels of fear—of a tame and cowardly spirit. The generous Zabdas will do me justice—nay, you all will—why am I apprehensive ?   Bear with me a moment more—

Queen and others.—Say on, say on, noble Otho.

Otho.—The great Longinus has said that it is needful that there be one empire at least in the world to stand between Rome and universal dominion.   I believe it. And that Palmyra may be, or continue to be, that kingdom, I counsel peace—I counsel delay—temporary concessions—negotiations—anything but war.   A Roman Emperor lives not forever; and let us once ward off the jealousy of Aurelian, by yielding to some of his demands, and resigning pretensions which are nothing in reality, but exist as names and shadows only, and long years of peace and prosperity may again arise, when our now infant kingdom may shoot up into the strong

bone and muscle of a more vigorous manhood, and with
reason assert rights which now it seems but madness,
essential madness, to do. Listen, great Queen! to the
counsels of a time-worn soldier, whose whole soul is bound
up in most true-hearted devotion to your greatness and
glory. I quarrel not with your ambition or your love
of warlike fame. I would only direct them to fields
where they may pluck fresh laurels, and divert them
from those where waits—pardon me, my royal mistress!
—inevitable shame.

Zabdas (springing to his feet).—Were not the words
which we have just heard the words of Otho, I would
cry out, Treason! treason! But Otho—is Otho. What
nation would ever, O Queen! outgrow its infancy, were
a policy like this now descanted upon to guide its counsels? The general who risks nothing can win nothing.
And the nation that should wait till absolutely sure of
victory before unsheathing the sword would never draw
it, or only in some poor skirmish, where victory would
be as disgraceful as defeat. Besides, although such a
nation were to rise by such victories, if victories those
may be called won by a thousand over an hundred,
who would not blush to own himself a citizen of it?
Greatness lies not in pounds weight of flesh, but in skill,
courage, warlike genius, energy, and an indomitable
will. A great heart will scatter a multitude. The love
of freedom in a few brave spirits overthrows kingdoms.
It was not, if I rightly remember, numbers by which
the Persian hosts were beaten upon the plains of Greece.
It was there something like three hundred to a million—
the million weighed more than the three hundred, yet
the three hundred were the heavier. The arm of one
Spartan fell like a tempest upon the degenerate Per-

sians, crushing its thousands at a single sweep. It was a great heart and a trusting spirit that made it weigh so against mere human flesh. Are we to wait till Pal·myra be as multitudinous as Rome ere we risk a battle? Perhaps Rome will grow as fast as Palmyra—and how long must we then wait? I care not though Aurelian bring half Europe at his back. There sits a throned spirit who will drive him back shattered and bleeding, the jest and ridicule of the observing world. She who, by the force of pure intellect, has out of this speck in the desert made a large empire, who has humbled Persia, and entered her capital in triumph, has defeated three Roman armies, and wrested more provinces than time will allow me to number, from the firm grasp of the self-styled mistress of the world—this more than Semira-mis is to be daunted, forsooth, because a Roman soldier of fortune sends his hirelings here and asks of her the surrender of three-fourths of her kingdom; she is to kneel and cry him mercy, and humbly lay ac his royal feet the laurels won by so much precious blood and treasure! May the sands of the desert bury Palmyra and her Queen, sooner than one humiliating word shall pass those lips, or one act of concession blast a fame to this hour spotless as the snows of Ararat, and bright as the Persian god. Shame upon the man who, after the lessons of the past, wants faith in his sovereign. Great Queen, believe me, the nation is with you. Palmyra, as one man, will pour out treasure to the last and least dust of gold, and blood to the last drop, that you may still sit secure upon that throne, and stretch your sceptre over a yet wider and undishonored empire.

    Otho.—Let not the Queen, let not the Queen doubt my faith—

Queen.—I doubt it not, good Otho. Heed not the sharp words of the impetuous Zabdas; in his zeal for the art he only loves and for his Queen, he has thrust his lance hither and thither at all adventures, but as in the sports of the field, he means no injury.

Otho.—Zabdas intends no wrong, I am well assured. I would only add a word to show upon what I ground my doubt of good success should Aurelian muster all his strength. It cannot be thought that I have lost my faith in the military genius and prowess of either Zenobia or Zabdas, with both of whom, side by side, I have fought so many times, and by their conduct mounted up to victory. Neither do I doubt the courage of our native Palmyrenes, nor their devotion to the interests of their country. They will war to the death. But should a second army be to be raised, should the chosen troops of the city and its neighboring territories be once cut off, upon whom are we then to rely? Where are the auxiliaries whom we can trust? What reliance can be placed upon Arabs, the Armenians, the Saracens, the Cappadocians, the Syrians? Is our empire so old, and so well molded into one mass, so single in interest and affection, that these scattered tribes—formerly hostile to each other and to us, many, most of them at different times subject to Rome—may be depended upon as our own people? Have we legions already drawn from their numbers, disciplined, and accustomed to our modes of warfare? Truly, this war with Rome seems to be approached much as if it were but some passing show of arms, some holiday pastime. But the gods grant that none of my forebodings turn true!

Zenobia.—It was my wish, before the final decision of the Senate and the Council, to receive from my friends, iu social confidence, a full expression of their feelings, their opinions, their hopes, and their fears, concerning the present posture of our affairs. My wish has been gratified, and I truly thank you all. It cannot be said that I blindly rushed upon danger and ruin, if these await us, or weakly blundered upon a wider renown, if that, as I doubt not, is to be the event of the impending contest. I would neither gain nor lose but as the effect of a wise calculation and a careful choice of means. Believe that now, as ever before, I discern with a clear eye the path which is to conduct us to a yet higher pitch of glory. I long ago anticipated the emergency that has arisen. I prepared then for the crisis which has come not till now. I am ready now. My armies are in complete discipline, the city itself so fortified with every art and muniment of war as safely to defy any power that any nation may array before its walls. I am advised to avert this evil by negotiation, by delay. Does any one believe that delay on our part will change the time-engendered character of Rome? If I cease to oppose, will Rome cease to be ambitious? Believe it not. The storm that threatens might be so warded off. perhaps, for a day—a month—a year—a reign—but after that it would come, and in all reasonable calculation, with tenfold fury.

I am charged with pride and ambition. The charge is true, and I glory in its truth. Who ever achieved anything great in letters, arts, or arms who was not ambitious? Cæsar was not more ambitious than Cicero. It was but in another way. All greatness is born of ambition. Let the ambition be a noble one, and who shall blame it? I confess I did once aspire to be Queen not only of Palmyra, but of the East. That I am. I

now aspire to remain so. Is it not an honorable ambition? Rome has the West. Let Palmyra possess the
East. Not that nature prescribes this, and no more
[*rising in enthusiasm*]; the gods prospering, and I swear
not that the Mediterranean shall hem me in upon the
west, or Persia on the east. Longinus is right: I would
that the world were mine. I feel within the will and
the power to bless it were it so.

Are not my people happy? I look upon the past and
the present, upon my nearer and remoter subjects, and
ask, nor fear the answer—Whom have I wronged? What
province have I oppressed? What city pillaged? What
region drained with taxes? Whose life have I unjustly
taken, or estates coveted or robbed? Whose honor have
I wantonly assailed? Whose rights, though of the
weakest and poorest, have I trenched upon? I dwell,
where I would ever dwell—in the hearts of my people.
It is writ in your faces that I reign not more over you
than within you. The foundation of my throne is not
more power than love. Suppose now my ambition add
another province to our realm? Is it an evil? The
kingdoms already bound to us by the joint acts of our-
self and the late royal Odenatus we found discordant
and at war. They are now united and at peace. One
harmonious whole has grown out of hostile and sundered
parts. At my hands they receive a common justice and
equal benefits. The channels of their commerce have
I opened, and dug them deep and sure. Prosperity and
plenty are in all their borders. The streets of our capital bear testimony to the distant and various industry
which here seeks its market. This is no vain boast-
ing—receive it not so, good friends: it is but truth.
He who traduces himself, sins with him who traduces

another. He who is unjust to himself, or less than just, breaks a law as well as he who hurts his neighbor. I tell you what I am and what I have done, that your trust for the future may not rest upon ignorant grounds.

If I am more than just to myself, rebuke me. If I have overstepped the modesty that became me, I am open to your censure and will bear it. But I have spoken that you may know your Queen—not only by her acts, but by her admitted principles. I tell you then that I am ambitious—that I crave dominion, and while I live will reign. Sprung from a line of kings, a throne is my natural seat. I love it. But I strive, too—you can bear me witness that I do—that it shall be, while I sit upon it, an honored, unpolluted seat. If I can, I will hang a yet brighter glory around it.

But see! the Roman Ambassadors approach: let us forth and meet them in the council hall. *Exeunt.*

WM. WARE.

CHRISTMAS-TIDE.

SCENE I.—Evening.

A room of poverty. Candle dimly burning. Bed on the floor. Stockings hanging near. Child speaks to her mother.

Child.

THEY say to-night is Christmas Eve, and, high as I
    could reach,
I've hung my stockings on the wall, and left a kiss on
    each.
I left a kiss on each for Him who'll fill my stockings
    quite:
He never came before, but oh, I'm sure He will to-night.

And to-morrow'll be the day our blessed Christ was born,
Who came on earth to pity me, whom many others scorn.

And why it is they treat me so indeed I can not tell,
But while I love Him next to you, then all seems wise
and well.

I long have looked for Christmas, mother,—waited all
the year;
And very strange it is indeed to feel its dawn so near;
But to-morrow 'll be the day I so have prayed to see,
And I long to sleep and wake, and find what it will
bring to me.

The snow is in the street, and through the window all
the day
I 've watched the little children pass: they seemed so
glad and gay!
And gayly did they talk about the gifts they would
receive;—
Oh, all the world is glad to-night, for this is Christmas
Eve!

And, mother, on the cold, cold floor I 've put my little
shoe,—
The other 's torn across the toe, and things might there
slip through;
I 've set my little shoe, mother, and it for you shall be,
For I know that He 'll remember you while He remem-
bers me.

So lay me in my bed, mother, and hear my prayers aright.
He never came before, but oh, I 'm sure He will to-night.

[*Curtain drops.*]

Scene II.—Midnight.

Mother knitting or mending. Child in night-dress sits erect in bed.
Child.

Mother, is it the morning yet? I dreamed that it was
here;

I thought the sun shone through the pane, so blessed and
so clear.
I dreamed my little stockings there were full as they
could hold.
But it's hardly morning yet, mother,—it is so dark and
cold.

I dreamed the bells rang from the church where the
happy people go,
And they rang good-will to all men in a language that I
know.
I thought I took from off the wall my little stockings
there,
And on the floor I emptied them,—such sights there
never were!

A doll was in there, meant for me, just like those little
girls
Who always turn away from me; and oh, it had *such*
curls!
I kissed it on its painted cheek; my own are not so sweet,
Though people used to stop to pat and praise them in
the street.

And, mother, there were many things that would have
pleased you, too ;
For He who had remembered me had not forgotten you.
But I only dreamed 't was morning, and yet 't is far away,
Though well I know that He will come before the early
day.
So I will put my dream aside, though I know my dream
was true,
And sleep, and dream my dream again, and rise at morn
with you.

[*Curtain drops.*]

SCENE III.—Christmas Morn.

Mother sitting at table, head resting on her hand.

Mother.

All night have I waked with weeping till the bells are
ringing wild,

All night have I waked with my sorrow, and lain in my
     tears, like a child.
For over against the wall, as empty as they can be,
The limp little stockings hang, and my heart is breaking
     in me!

Your vision was false as the world, oh, darling dreamer
     and dear!
And how can I bear you to wake, and find no Christmas
     here?
Better you and I were asleep in the slumber whence none
     may start.
And oh, those empty stockings! I could fill them out
     of my heart!

No Christmas for you or for me, darling; your kisses
     were all in vain;
I have given your kisses back to you over and over again;
I have folded you to my breast with a moaning no one
     hears:
Your heart is happy in dreams, though your hair is damp
     with my tears.

I am out of heart and hope; I am almost out of my mind;
The world is cruel and cold, and only Christ is kind;
And much must be borne and forborne; but the heaviest
     burden of all
That ever hath lain on my life are those little light things
     on the wall.

The bells have ceased their ringing, and—footsteps ap-
     proach my door!
     (*Door opens, and a basket of food, a bundle of clothing,
     and toys for the little girl brought in.*)

Dear Lord, thou hast not forgotten, for some one remem-
     bers the poor.
     (*The gifts are displayed. The daughter appears.*)
For me and mine these treasures! Have my eyes mis-
     taken the light?

The sun will now shine warmer, and the fire burn brighter to-night.

ADAPTED FROM A. W. BELLAW BY J. W. SHOEMAKER.

AUNT BETSEY AND LITTLE DAVY.

From Dickens' David Copperfield.

CHARACTERS.

AUNT BETSEY.—A lady of sixty, with gray hair, rather handsome features, quick, bright eye, slender, straight, active, and peculiar—dress of black or lavender, with plain, narrow, untrimmed skirt, low shoes, turn-down linen collar and cuffs, short, plain apron, white cap with high front frill, over which is tied a large silk handkerchief; pair of gardening gloves and gardening knife in hand.

DAVID.—Slender, timid child of nine or ten years; in first scene, with face, hands, and neck sun browned, shirt, trowsers, and hat and shoes soiled and torn, features and clothing covered with chalk-like dust.

MR. DICK.—A fleshy, florid, smiling, gray-haired man of forty, with high standing collar and stiff, wide cravat, loose gray coat and waistcoat, white trousers; somewhat stooped at the neck, one eye frequently closed, watch in fob, money loose in pocket, and for which he shows his fondness by frequent jingling.

JANET.—Plump, healthy, good-natured servant girl, clad in neat, figured muslin dress.

MR. MURDSTONE.—In suit of black, high silk hat, black hair and heavy black whiskers, lowering black eye-brows, thin lips, pressed close together; deep, hard voice.

MISS MURDSTONE.—Much resembling her brother in features and voice, clad in plain, black riding dress, close bonnet, with veil thrown back; she carries a parasol and a bag with a heavy chain and clasp.

SCENE I.

Room in Aunt Betsey's house, tastefully furnished with sofa, table, chairs, screen, etc.

Curtain rises.—Aunt Betsey discovered at an open door, and Davy in his woe-begone condition standing timidly before her.

Aunt B. (shaking her head and making a chop in the

air with her knife).—Go away! Go along, I say! No boys here!

David (timidly looking up and touching her hand with his finger).—If you please, ma'am. [*Aunt B. starts.*] If you please, aunt.

Aunt B. (amazedly).—Eh?

David.—If you please, aunt, I am your nephew!

Aunt B. (sitting flat down in doorway).—Mercy on us! Mercy on us!

David.—I am David Copperfield, of Blunderstone, in Suffolk, where you came after my papa died, on the night when I was born, and saw my dear mamma. Two or three years before mamma died she was married to a Mr. Murdstone—he had a sister who lived with us— they were both very cruel to me. I have been very unhappy since dear mamma died. I have been slighted, and taught nothing, and thrown upon myself, and put to work not fit for me. It made me run away to you. [*Breaking into sobs.*] I was robbed at first setting out, and have walked all the way, and have never slept in a bed since I began the journey.

Aunt B. (rises, seizes David by the collar, brings him into the room, unlocks a cabinet, takes out large bottles and administers three or four different kinds of medicines as restoratives, exclaiming at intervals).—Mercy on us! Mercy on us! [*She then places David upon the sofa, puts a shawl under his head, takes off handkerchief from her own head and places it under his feet to prevent him from soiling the cover, then rings bell. Enter servant.*]

Aunt B.—Janet, go up-stairs, give my compliments to my friend, Mr. Dick, and say I wish to speak to him.

[*Exit Janet, looking with surprised air at child on sofa.*]

Aunt B. (seating herself behind screen).—Mercy on us! Mercy on us! Mercy on us!

[*Enter Mr. Dick, smiling.*]

Aunt B.—Mr. Dick, don't be a fool, because nobody can be more discreet than you can, when you choose. We all know that. So don't be a fool, whatever you are. You have heard me mention David Copperfield? Now, don't pretend not to have a memory, because you and I know better.

Mr. Dick.—David Copperfield? David Copperfield? Oh, yes, to be sure. David, certainly.

Aunt B.—Well, this is his boy, his son. He would be as like his father as it's possible to be, if he was not so like his mother, too.

Mr. Dick (smiling).—His son? David's son? Indeed!

Aunt B.—Yes, and he has done a pretty piece of business. He has run away. Ah! His sister, Betsey Trotwood, if there had been a sister, never would have run away.

Mr. Dick.—Oh! you think she wouldn't have run away?

Aunt B.—Bless and save the man! how he talks! Don't I know she wouldn't? She would have lived with her godmother, and we should have been devoted to one another. Where, in the name of wonder, should his sister, Betsey Trotwood, have run from, or to?

Mr. Dick.—Nowhere.

Aunt B.—Well, then, how can you pretend to be wool-gathering, Dick, when you are as sharp as a surgeon's lancet? Now, here you see young David Copperfield, and the question I put to you is, what shall I do with him?

Mr. Dick (scratching his head feebly).—What shall you do with him? Oh! do with him?

Aunt B. (holding up her forefinger).—Yes. Come! I want some very sound advice.

Mr. Dick.—Why, if I was you, I should—I should wash him!

Aunt B.—Janet, Mr. Dick sets us all right. Heat the bath!

[*Exit Janet.*]

Aunt B. (looking out of door or window, calling excitedly).—Janet! Janet! Donkeys! Drive them off! They sha'n't trespass on my green! Now, Mr. Dick, whatever do you suppose possessed that poor unfortunate Baby, that she must go and be married again?

Mr. Dick.—Perhaps she fell in love with her second husband.

Aunt B.—Fell in love! What do you mean? What business had she to do it?

Mr. Dick (simpering).—Perhaps she did it for pleas-ure.

Aunt B.—Pleasure, indeed! A mighty pleasure for the poor Baby to fix her simple faith upon any dog of a fellow, certain to ill-use her in some way or other. What did she propose to herself, I should like to know! She had had one husband. She had seen David Copperfield out of the world, who was always running after wax dolls from his cradle. And then, as if this was not enough, she marries a second time—goes and marries a murderer—or a man with a name like it—and stands in this child's light! And the natural consequence is, as anybody but a baby might have foreseen, that he prowls and wanders. He's as like Cain before he was grown up as he can be. [*Calling.*] Janet! Donkeys—donkeys!

Now, Mr. Dick [*forefinger up*], I am going to ask you another question. Look at this child.

Mr. Dick.—David's son?

Aunt B.—Exactly so. What would you do with him?

Mr. Dick.—Do with David's son?

Aunt B.—Ah, with David's son.

Mr. Dick.—Oh! Yes. Do with—I should—I should, after the bath, give him his supper and put him to bed.

[*Re-enter Janet.*]

Aunt B.—Janet, Mr. Dick sets us all right. Arrange the bed in the room overlooking the sea. Prepare the supper and I will see that the child has a bath.

[CURTAIN.]

SCENE II.

Aunt Betsey seated at breakfast table profoundly meditating. David, very cleanly washed and nicely combed, fitted out in some of Mr. Dick's clothes, which are far too large for him, with a shawl tied round his shoulders, is also seated at table and bashfully endeavoring to eat his breakfast.

Aunt B.—Hallo! [*David looks up respectfully.*] I have written to him.

David.—To?

Aunt B.—To your father-in-law. I have sent him a letter that I'll trouble him to attend to, or he and I will fall out, I can tell him!

David.—Does he know where I am, aunt?

Aunt B.—I have told him, and I expect him here shortly.

David.—Oh! I can't think what I shall do if I have to go back to Mr. Murdstone!

Aunt B.—I don't know anything about it. I can't

say, I am sure. We shall see. I wish you would go
up-stairs and give my compliments to Mr. Dick, and
I'll be glad to know how he gets on with his Memorial.
[*Exit David.*]

(*Aunt Betsey rings bell, rises, goes to work-basket, seats
herself, threads needle, and begins to sew. Janet enters,
carries away dishes, and arranges room.*)

Aunt B. (*soliloquizing*).—How I wish that Murderer,
or Murdstone, or whatever you call him, would make
his appearance just now. I am in a mood to say
some things he won't like. The statements I have, from
time to time, drawn from the child go to prove that he
has been more shamefully treated than I at first was led
to believe. [*Re-enter David.*] Well, child, and what
of Mr. Dick, this morning?

David.—He sends his compliments, and says he is
getting on very well indeed.

Aunt B.—And what do you think of Mr. Dick.
[*David hesitating.*] Come! Your sister, ·Betsey Trotwood—if there had been a Betsey Trotwood—would
have told me what she thought of any one directly. Be
as like your sister would have been as you can, and
speak out!

David.—Is he—is Mr. Dick—I ask because I don't
know, aunt—is he at all out of his mind, then?

Aunt B.—Not a morsel.

David.—Oh! (*Timidly.*)

Aunt B.—If there is anything in the world that Mr.
Dick is not, it's that.

David.—Oh!

Aunt B.—He has been called mad. I have a selfish
pleasure in saying he has been called mad, or I should
not have had the benefit of his society and advice for

these last ten years and upward—in fact, ever since your sister, Betsey Trotwood, disappointed me.

David.—So long as that?

Aunt B.—And nice people they were, who had the audacity to call him mad. Mr. Dick is a sort of distant connection of mine; it doesn't matter how; I needn't enter into that. If it hadn't been for me, his own brother would have shut him up for life. That's all. Janet! Donkeys! donkeys! [*Springing to her feet and rushing to the door.*] Go along with you. [*Shaking her fist.*] How dare you trespass? Go along! Oh, you bold-faced thing!

David.—That is Miss Murdstone, aunt.

Aunt B.—I don't care who it is. I won't be trespassed upon. I won't allow it. Go away! Janet, turn him round. Lead him off!

David.—Shall I go away, aunt?

Aunt B.—No, sir. Certainly not. (*Pushing David into a corner near her and fencing him in with a chair.*)

[*Enter Mr. and Miss Murdstone.*]

Aunt B.—Oh! I was not aware at first to whom I had the pleasure of objecting. But I don't allow anybody to ride over that turf. I make no exceptions. I don't allow anybody to do it.

Miss M.—Your regulation is rather awkward to strangers.

Aunt B.—Is it?

Mr. M.—Miss Trotwood!

Aunt B.—I beg your pardon. You are the Mr. Murdstone who married the widow of my late nephew, David Copperfield, of Blunderstone Rookery?

Mr. M.—I am.

Aunt B.—You'll excuse my saying, sir, that I think

it would have been a much better and happier thing if you had left that poor child alone.

Miss M.—I so far agree with what Miss Trotwood has remarked, that I consider our lamented Clara to have been, in all essential respects, a mere child.

Aunt B.—It is a comfort to you and me, ma'am, who are getting on in life, and are not likely to be made unhappy by our personal attractions, that nobody can say the same of us.

Miss M.—No doubt! And it certainly might have been, as you say, a better and happier thing for my brother if he had never entered into such a marriage. I have always been of that opinion.

Aunt B.—I have no doubt you have. [*Enter Mr. Dick, who stands by table, jingles money, and looks rather foolish.*] This is Mr. Dick, an old and intimate friend, on whose judgment I frequently rely. (*Mr. and Miss Murdstone bow stiffly without rising.*)

Mr. M.—Miss Trotwood, on the receipt of your letter, I considered it an act of great justice to myself, and perhaps of more respect to you—

Aunt B.—Thank you. You needn't mind me.

Mr. M.—To answer it in person, however inconvenient the journey, rather than by letter. This unhappy boy, who has run away from his friends and his occupation—

Miss M. (interrupting).—And whose appearance [*pointing toward David*] is perfectly scandalous and disgraceful.

Mr. M.—Jane Murdstone, have the goodness not to interrupt me. This unhappy boy, Miss Trotwood, has been the occasion of much domestic trouble and uneasiness, both during the lifetime of my late dear wife and since. He has a sullen, rebellious spirit, a violent temper, and an untoward, intractable disposition. Both

my sister and myself have endeavored to correct his
vices, but ineffectually. And I have felt—we both have
felt, I may say, my sister being fully in my confidence—
that it is right you should receive this grave and dis-
passionate assurance from our lips.

Miss M.—It can hardly be necessary for me to con-
firm anything stated by my brother, but I beg to observe,
that of all the boys in the world, I believe this is the
worst boy.

Aunt B. (shortly).—Strong.

Miss M.—But not at all too strong for the facts.

Aunt B.—Ha! Well, sir?

Mr. M.—I have my own opinions, and more, as to the
best mode of bringing him up; they are founded, in part,
on my knowledge of him, and in part on my knowledge
of my own means and resources. I am responsible for
them to myself, I act upon them, and I say no more
about them. It is enough that I place this boy under
the eye of a friend of my own, in a respectable business;
that it does not please him; that he runs away from it;
makes himself a common vagabond about the country;
and comes here in rags to appeal to you, Miss Trotwood.
I wish to set before you, honorably, the exact con-
sequences—so far as they are within my knowledge—of
your abetting him in this appeal.

Aunt B.—But about the respectable business first.
If he had been your own boy, you would have put him
to it just the same, I suppose?

Miss M.—If he had been my brother's own boy his
character, I trust, would have been altogether different.

Aunt B.—Or if the poor child, his mother, had been
alive, he would still have gone into the respectable business, would he?

Mr. M.—I believe that Clara would have disputed nothing which myself and my sister, Jane Murdstone, were agreed was for the best.

[*Miss M. murmuring audibly.*]

Aunt B.—Humph! Unfortunate baby! The poor child's annuity died with her?

Mr. M.—Died with her.

Aunt B.—And there was no settlement of the little property—the house and garden—the what's-its-name Rookery without any rooks in it—upon her boy?

Mr. M.—It had been left to her unconditionally by her first husband.

Aunt B.—Of course it was left to her unconditionally. But when she married again—when she took that most disastrous step of marrying you, in short, to be plain—did no one put in a word for the boy at that time?

Mr. M.—My late wife loved her second husband, madam, and trusted implicitly in him.

Aunt B.—Your late wife, sir, was a most unworldly, most unhappy, most unfortunate baby. (*Shaking her head at him.*) That's what she was. And now, what have you got to say next?

Mr. M.—Merely this, Miss Trotwood. I am here to take David back; to take him back unconditionally, to dispose of him as I think proper, and to deal with him as I think right. I am not here to make any promise, or give any pledge to anybody. If you step in between him and me now, you must step in, Miss Trotwood, forever. I cannot trifle, or be trifled with. I am here, for the first and last time, to take him away. Is he ready to go? If he is not—and you tell me he is not; on any pretense; it is indifferent to me what—my doors are shut against him henceforth, and yours, I take it for granted, are open to him.

Aunt B.—Well, ma'am, have you got anything to remark?

Miss M.—Indeed, Miss Trotwood, all that I could say has been so well said by my brother, and all that I know to be the fact has been so plainly stated by him, that I have nothing to add except my thanks for your politeness [*sarcastically*]—for your very great politeness, I am sure.

Aunt B.—And what does the boy say? Are you ready to go, David?

David (*piteously*).—Please, aunt, don't let them take me. They have never been kind to me; they made mamma, who always loved me dearly, very unhappy about me, and they made my life so miserable. Please, aunt, keep me and befriend me for my papa's sake.

Aunt B.—Mr. Dick, what shall I do with this child?

Mr. Dick (*hesitating and brightening*).—Have him measured for a suit of clothes directly.

Aunt B.—Mr. Dick, give me your hand [*shaking Mr. Dick's hand cordially and drawing David to her*], for your common sense is invaluable. [*To Mr. Murdstone.*] You can go when you like; I'll take my chance with the boy. If he's all you say he is, at least I can do as much for him then as you have done. But I don't be-lieve a word of it.

Mr. M. (*rising*).—Miss Trotwood, if you were a gen-tleman—

Aunt B.—Stuff and nonsense! Don't talk to me!

Miss M. (*rising*).—How exquisitely polite! Over powering, really!

Aunt B. (*rising*).—Do you think I don't know what

kind of life you must have led that poor, unhappy, mis-
directed baby? Do you think I don't know what a
woeful day it was for the soft little creature when you
first came in her way—smirking and making great eyes
at her, I'll be bound, as if you couldn't say buh! to a
goose.

Miss M.—I never heard anything so elegant!

Aunt B.—Do you think I can't understand you as
well as if I had seen you, now that I do see and hear
you—which I tell you, candidly, is anything but a
pleasure to me? Oh, yes, bless us! who so smooth and
silky as Mr. Murdstone at first! The poor benighted
innocent had never seen such a man. He was made of
sweetness. He worshiped her! He doted on her boy—
tenderly doted on him! He was to be another father
to him, and they were all to live together in a garden of
roses, weren't they?

Miss M.—I never heard anything like this person in
my life.

Aunt B.—And when you had made sure of the poor
little fool, God forgive me that I should call her so, and
she gone where you won't go in a hurry—because you
had not done wrong enough to her and hers, you must
begin to train her, must you? Begin to break her, like
a poor caged bird, and wear her deluded life away in
teaching her to sing your notes?

Miss M.—This is either insanity or intoxication, and
my suspicion is that it's intoxication.

Aunt B. (not heeding interruption).—Mr. Murdstone,
you were a tyrant to the simple baby, and you broke
her heart. She was a loving baby—I know that; I
knew it years before you ever saw her—and through the
best part of her weakness you gave her the wounds she

died of. There is the truth for your comfort, however you like it. And you and your instruments may make the most of it.

Miss M.—Allow me to inquire, Miss Trotwood, whom you are pleased to call, in a choice of words in which I am not experienced, my brother's instruments?

Aunt B. (unheeding Miss M.).—It was clear enough, as I have told you, years before you ever saw her—and why in the mysterious dispensations of Providence you ever did see her, is more than humanity can comprehend—it was clear enough that the poor, soft little thing would marry somebody, at sometime or other; but I did hope it wouldn't have been as bad as it has turned out. That was the time, Mr. Murdstone, when she gave birth to her boy here, to the poor child you sometimes tormented her through afterward, which is a disagreeable remembrance, and makes the sight of him odious now. Aye! aye! you needn't wince! I know it's true without that. And now, good-day, and good-bye! Good-day to you, too, ma'am. Let me see you ride a donkey over my green again, and as sure as you have a head upon your shoulders I'll knock your bonnet off and tread upon it.

[*Miss M. places her arm through her brother's and they walk haughtily out of the door.*]

David.—Oh, aunt, I thank you very, very much, and I shall try hard to be a good boy and give you no trouble. [*Places his arms around his aunt's neck and kisses her. Mr. Dick laughs heartily, jingles his money, and shakes hands with David.*]

Aunt B.—You'll consider yourself guardian, jointly with me, of this child, Mr. Dick?

Mr. Dick.—I shall be delighted to be the guardian of David's son.

Aunt B.—Very good, that's settled. I have been thinking, do you know, Mr. Dick, that I might call him Trotwood?

Mr. Dick.—Certainly, certainly. Call him Trotwood, certainly. David's son's Trotwood.

Aunt B.—Trotwood Copperfield, you mean.

Mr. Dick.—Yes, to be sure. Yes. Trotwood Copperfield.

Aunt B.—And the suit of new clothes which I shall purchase this afternoon shall be marked in indelible ink—and in my own handwriting—Trotwood Copperfield. Moreover, I shall put the boy to school and give him an education. Henceforth, Trotwood (*kindly and proudly*), you are to be my boy, and no murdering Murdstones will have a chance to practice on you again while Aunt Betsey Trotwood holds a place in this world.

[CURTAIN.]

Dramatized by MRS. J. W. SHOEMAKER.

THE MURDER OF THOMAS À BECKET.

Adapted from Tennyson's Tragedy—Becket.

EFFECTIVE EITHER AS A READING OR A DIALOGUE.

Thomas à Becket, Archbishop of Canterbury, was a man of great talent and fearless courage, but he unwisely set himself against all propositions of the King tending to regulate, or make ecclesiastical authority subservient to civil power. So determined was he in his opposition, that finally Henry, though one of the Archbishop's firmest friends, in a fit of impatience, was led to exclaim: "Is there no one of my subjects who will rid me of this insolent priest?" Four knights, enemies of à Becket, construing this as a command, proceeded to the residence of the prelate, and pursuing him into the Cathedral, barbarously slew him before the altar A. D. 1170.

DRAMATIS PERSONÆ.

THOMAS À BECKET, Archbishop of Canterbury.

GRIM, a monk of Cambridge, } Friends of à Becket.
JOHN of Salisbury,

SIR REGINALD FITZURSE, }
SIR RICHARD DE BRITO, | The four knights of the King's house-
SIR WILLIAM DE TRACY, | hold and enemies of à Becket.
SIR HUGH DE MORVILLE, }

MONKS.

For costumes, consult history and historic scenes of the time of
Henry II.

SCENE.

*Altar and chancel of a Cathedral. A concealed chorus of
voices indicative of monks chanting the service. En-
trance right and left.*

*Becket (entering, forced along by John of Salisbury and
Grim).—*   No, I tell you!
I cannot bear a hand upon my person,
Why do you force me thus against my will?
Grim.—
My lord, we force you from your enemies.
Becket.—
As you would force a king from being crown'd.
John of Salisbury.—
We must not force the crown of martyrdom.
                 [*Service stops. Enter Monks*
Monks.—
Here is the great Archbishop! He lives! he lives'
Die with him, and be glorified together.
Becket.—
Together? . . . get you back! go on with the office.
Monks.—
Come, then, with us to vespers.
Becket.—   How can I come
When you so block the entry? Back, I say!

Go on with the office. Shall not Heaven be served
Tho' earth's last earthquake clash'd the minstel-
    bells,
And the great deeps were broken up again,
And hiss'd against the sun?   [*Noise in the cloisters.*
Monks.—   The murderers, hark!
    Let us hide! let us hide!
Becket.—   What do these people fear?
Monks.—
    Those arm'd men in the cloister.
Becket.—   Be not such cravens!
    I will go out and meet them.
Grim and others.—
    Fly, fly, my lord, before they burst the doors!
                                   [*Knocking.*
Becket.—

Why, these are our own monks who follow'd us!
Undo the doors: the church is not a castle:
Knock, and it shall be open'd.   Are you deaf?
What, have I lost authority among you?
Stand by, make way!
                  [*Opens the doors.   Enter Monks.*
                  Come in, my friends, come in!
Nay, faster, faster!
Monks.—   Oh, my lord Archbishop,
A score of Knights all arm'd with swords and
    axes—
To the choir, to the choir!
           [*Monks divide part to the right, part to the left.
            The rush of these last bears Becket along
            with them some distance, where he is left
            standing alone.*
Becket.—   Shall I too pass to the choir,

And die upon the Patriarchal throne
Of all my predecessors?
John of Salisbury.—   No, to the crypt!
Twenty steps down.   Stumble not in the darkness,
Lest they should seize thee.
Grim.—   To the crypt? no—no,
To the chapel of St. Blaise beneath the roof!
John of Salisbury (pointing upward and downward).—
That way, or this!   Save thyself either way.
Becket.—
Oh, no, not either way, nor any way
Save by that way which leads thro' night to light.
Not twenty steps, but one.
And fear not I should stumble in the darkness,
Not tho' it be their hour, the power of darkness,
But my hour too, the power of light in darkness!
I am not in the darkness but the light,
Seen by the Church in Heaven, the Church on
     earth—
The power of life in death to make her free!
                    [*Enter the four knights.*
Fitzurse.—
Here, here, King's men!
               [*Catches hold of the last flying Monk.*
                    Where is the traitor Becket?
Monk.—
I am not he, I am not he, my lord.
I am not he indeed!
Fitzurse.—   Hence to the fiend!
                    [*Pushes him away.*
Where is this treble traitor to the King?
De Tracy.—
Where is the Archbishop, Thomas Becket?

Becket.—   Here.
No traitor to the King, but Priest of God,
Primate of England.   [*Descending into the transept*
                              I am he ye seek.
What would ye have of me?
Fitzurse.—   Your life.
De Tracy.—   Your life.
De Morville.—
Save that you will absolve the bishops.
Becket.—   Never,—
Except they make submission to the Church.
You had my answer to that cry before.
De Morville.—
Why, then you are a dead man; flee!
Becket.—   I will not.
I am readier to be slain, than thou to slay.
Hugh, I know well thou hast but half a heart
To bathe this sacred pavement with my blood.
God pardon thee and these, but God's full curse
Shatter you all to pieces if ye harm
One of my flock!
Fitzurse.—   Was not the great gate shut?
They are thronging in to vespers—half the town.
We shall be overwhelm'd. Seize him and carry
      him!
Come with us—nay—thou art our prisoner—come!
De Morville.—
Ay, make him prisoner, do not harm the man.

          [*Fitzurse lays hold of the Archbishop's pall.*

Becket.—
Touch me not!
De Brito.—   How the good priest gods himself!

Fitzurse.—

I will not only touch, but drag thee hence.

Becket.—

Thou art my man, thou art my vassal.   Away!

[Flings him off till he reels, almost to falling.

De Tracy (lays hold of the pall).—

Come; as he said, thou art our prisoner.

Becket.—   Down!

[Throws him headlong.

Fitzurse (advances with drawn sword).—

I told thee that I should remember thee!

Becket.—

Profligate pander!

Fitzurse.—   Do you hear that! strike! strike!

[Strikes off the Archbishop's mitre, and wounds
him in the forehead.

Becket (covers his eyes with his hand).—

I do commend my cause to God, the Virgin,

St. Denis of France and St. Alphege of England,

And all the tutelar Saints of Canterbury.

[Grim wraps his arms about the Archbishop.

Spare this defense, dear brother.

[Tracy has arisen, and approaches, hesitatingly,
with his sword raised.

Fitzurse.—   Strike him, Tracy!

Strike, I say.

Grim.—

O God, O noble knights, O sacrilege!

Strike our Archbishop in his own cathedral!

The Pope, the King will curse you—the whole
world

Abhor you; ye will die the death of dogs!

Nay, nay, good Tracy.   *[Lifts his arm.*

Fitzurse.—   Answer not, but strike.
De Tracy.—
    There is my answer then.
        [*Sword falls on Grim's arm, and glances from it,
            wounding Becket.*
Grim.—   Mine arm is sever'd.
    I can no more—fight out the good fight—die
    Conqueror.   [*Staggers and falls.*
Becket (falling on his knees).—
        At the right hand of Power—
    Power and great glory—for thy Church, O Lord—
                              [*Sinks prone.*
De Brito.—
    This last to rid thee of a world of brawls! (*Kills
        him.*)
    The traitor's dead, and will arise no more.
Fitzurse.—
    Nay, have we still'd him? What! the great Arch-
        bishop!
    Does he breathe? No?
De Tracy.—   No, Reginald, he is dead.
            (*Storm bursts.*)*
De Morville.—
    Will the earth gape and swallow us?
De Brito.—   The deed's done—
    Away! Away!
        [*De Brito, De Tracy, Fitzurse, rush out, crying
            "King's men!" De Morville follows slowly.
            Flashes of lightning and sounds of thunder.*

---

* A tremendous thunderstorm actually broke over the Cathedral as the murderers were leaving it.

SCENE FROM THE LADY OF LYONS.

CHARACTERS. $\left\{\begin{array}{l}\text{CLAUDE MELNOTTE,}\\ \text{WIDOW MELNOTTE,}\\ \text{PAULINE.}\end{array}\right.$

Widow—So, I think that looks very neat. He sent me a line, so blotted that I can scarcely read it, to say he would be here almost immediately. She must have loved him well, indeed, to have forgotten his birth; for though he was introduced to her in disguise, he is too honorable not to have revealed to her the artifice; which her love only could forgive. Well, I do not wonder at it; for though my son is not a prince, he ought to be one, and that's almost as good. (*Knock at the door in* F.) Ah! here they are.

Enter MELNOTTE *and* PAULINE.

Widow—Oh, my boy; the pride of my heart! welcome, welcome! I beg pardon, ma'am, but I do love him so!

Pauline—Good woman, I really—why, Prince, what is this? Does the old lady know you? Oh, I guess, you have done her some service. Another proof of your kind heart, is it not?

Mel—Of my kind heart, ay!

Pauline—So you know the Prince?

Widow—Know him, madam? Ah, I begin to fear it is you who know him not!

Pauline—Can we stay here, my lord? I think there's something very wild about her.

Mel—Madam, I—no, I cannot tell her; what a coward is a man who has lost his honor! Speak to her—

speak to her (*to his mother*)—tell her that—O Heaven, that I were dead!

Pauline—How confused he looks!—this strange place!—this woman—what can it mean? I half suspect—Who are you madam! who are you? can't you speak? are you struck dumb?

Widow—Claude, you have not deceived her? Ah! shame upon you! I thought that before you went to the altar she was to have known all.

Pauline—All! what! my blood freezes in my veins!

Widow—Poor lady! dare I tell her, Claude? Know you not, then, madam, that this young man is of poor though honest parents? Know you not that you are wedded to my son, Claude Melnotte?

Pauline—Your son! hold—hold! do not speak to me. Is this a jest? is it? I know it is, only speak— one word—one look—one smile. I cannot believe—I, who love thee so—I cannot believe that thou art such a —No, I will not wrong thee by a harsh word—speak!

Mel—Leave us. Have pity on her, on me; leave us.

Widow—Oh, Claude, that I should live to see thee bowed by shame! thee, of whom I was so proud! [*Exit.*]

Pauline—Her son, her son!

Mel—Now, lady, hear me.

Pauline—Hear thee!
Ay, speak—her son! have fiends a parent? Speak,
That thou may'st silence curses—speak!

Mel—No, curse me;
Thy curse would blast me less than thy forgiveness.

Pauline—"This is thy palace, where the perfumed light
Steals through the mist of alabaster lamps,
And every air is heavy with the sighs

Of orange groves, and music from sweet lutes,
And murmurs of low fountains, that gush forth
I' the midst of roses ! " Dost thou like the picture ?
This is my bridal home, and *thou* my bridegroom.
O fool ! O dupe ! O wretch ! I see it all—
The by-word and the jeer of every tongue
In Lyons. Hast thou in thy heart one touch
Of human kindness ? If thou hast, why, kill me,
And save thy wife from madness. No, it cannot—
It cannot be ; this is some horrid dream ;
I shall wake soon. Art flesh ? art man ? or but
The shadows seen in sleep ? It is too real.
What have I done to thee ? How sinn'd against thee.
That thou should'st crush me thus ?

    Mel—Pauline, by pride
Angels have fallen, ere thy time : by pride—
That sole alloy of thy most lovely mould—
The evil spirit of a bitter love,
And a revengeful heart, had power upon thee.
From my first years my soul was fill'd with thee ;
I saw thee midst the flow'rs the lowly boy
Tended, unmark'd by thee—a spirit of bloom,
And joy, and freshness, as if Spring itself
Were made a living thing, and wore thy shape.
I saw thee, and the passionate heart of man
Entered the breast of the wild-dreaming boy.
And from that hour I grew—what, to the last
I shall be—thine adorer ! Well, this love,
Vain, frantic, guilty, if thou wilt, became
A fountain of ambition and bright hope ;
I thought of tales that, by the winter hearth
Old gossips tell—how maidens sprung from kings
Have stoop'd from their high sphere ; how love, like
        death,

Levels all ranks, and lays the shepherd's crook
Beside the sceptre.
My father died; and I, the peasant born,
Was my own lord. Then did I seek to rise
Out of the prison of my mean estate:
And, with such jewels as the exploring mind
Brings from the caves of knowledge, buy my ransom
From those twin gaolers of the daring heart—
Low birth and iron fortune. For thee I grew
A midnight student o'er the dreams of sages:
For thee I sought to borrow from each grace,
And every muse, such attributes as lend
Ideal charms to love. I thought of thee,
And passion taught me poesy—of thee,
And on the painter's canvass grew the life
Of beauty! Art became the shadow
Of the dear starlight of thy haunting eyes!
Men call'd me vain—some mad—I heeded not;
But still toil'd on—hoped on—for it was sweet,
If not to win, to feel more worthy thee?
    Pauline—Why do I cease to hate him?
    Mel—At last, in one mad hour, I dared to pour
The thoughts that burst their channels into song,
And sent them to thee—such a tribute, lady,
As beauty rarely scorns, even from the meanest.
The name appended by the burning heart
That long'd to shew its idol what bright things
It had created—yea, the enthusiast's name,
That should have been thy triumph, was thy scorn;
That very hour, when passion, turn'd to wrath,
Resembled hatred most—when thy disdain
Made my whole soul a chaos—in that hour
The tempters found me a revengeful tool

For their revenge! Thou hadst trampled on the worm—
It turned and stung thee!
Pauline—Love, sir, hath no sting.
What was the slight of a poor powerless girl
To the deep wrong of this most vile revenge?
Oh, how I loved this man! a serf, a slave!
   Mel—Hold, lady! No, not a slave! Despair is
   free!
I will not tell thee of the throes, the struggles,
The anguish, the remorse: no, let it pass!
And let me come to such most poor atonement
Yet in my power. Pauline!——
   Pauline—No, touch me not!
I know my fate. You are, by law, my tyrant,
And I—O Heaven!—a peasant's wife! I'll work,
Toil, drudge, do what thou wilt—but touch me not;
Let my wrongs make me sacred!
   Mel—Do not fear me.
Thou dost not know me, madam; at the altar
My vengeance ceased—my guilty oath expired!
Henceforth, no image of some marble saint
Niched in cathedral aisles is hallowed more
From the rude hand of sacrilegious wrong.
I am thy husband—nay, thou need'st not shudder;
Here at thy feet I lay a husband's rights.
A marriage thus unholy—unfulfilled—
A bond of fraud—is, by the laws of France,
Made void and null. To-night sleep—sleep in peace.
To-morrow, pure and virgin as this morn
I bore thee, bathed in blushes, from the shrine,
Thy father's arms shall take thee to thy home.
The law shall do thee justice, and restore
Thy right to bless another with thy love.

And when thou art happy, and hast half forgot
Him who so loved—so wrong'd thee, think, at least—
Heaven left some remnant of the angel still
In that poor peasant's nature.

              [Enter WIDOW.]

Conduct this lady—she is not my wife ;
She is our guest—our honored guest—my mother—
To the poor chamber where the sleep of virtue
Never, beneath my father's honest roof,
Ev'n villains dare to mar! Now, lady, now,
I think thou wilt believe me.

                            Go, my mother !

    Widow—She is not thy wife !
    Mel—Hush, hush ! for mercy's sake.
Speak not, but go.

    [Exit WIDOW. PAULINE *follows, turns to look back.*]
    Mel—All angels bless and guard her !

HENRY THE FIFTH'S WOOING.

K. HEN—Fair Katharine, and most fair,
    Will you vouchsafe to teach a soldier terms
Such as will enter at a lady's ear
And plead his love-suit to her gentle heart ?

    Kath—Your majesty shall mock at me ; I cannot
        speak your England.

    K. Hen—O fair Katharine, if you will love me soundly
with your French heart, I will be glad to hear you confess it brokenly with your English tongue. Do you like
me, Kate ?

    Kath—Pardonnez-moi, I cannot tell vat is 'like me.'

K. Hen—An angel is like you, Kate, and you are like an angel.

Kath—Que dit-il? que je suis semblable à les anges?

Alice—Oui, vraiment, sauf votre grace, ainsi dit-il.

K. Hen—I said so, dear Katharine; and I must not blush to affirm it.

Kath—O les langues hommes sont pleines de tromperies.

K. Hen—What says she, fair one? that the tongues of men are full of deceits?

Alice—Oui, dat de tongues of de mans is be full of deceits : dat is de princess.

K. Hen—The princess is the better English woman. I' faith, Kate, my wooing is fit for thy understanding: I am glad thou canst speak no better English; for, if thou couldst, thou wouldst find me such a plain king that thou wouldst think I had sold my farm to buy my crown. I know no ways to mince it in love, but directly to say 'I love you:' then if you urge me further than to say 'do you in faith?' I wear out my suit. Give me your answer; i' faith, do: and so clap hands and a bargain: how say you, lady?

Kath—Sauf votre honneur, me understand vell.

K. Hen—Marry, if you would put me to verses or to dance for your sake, Kate, why you undid me: for the one I have neither words nor measures, and for the other, I have no strength in measure, yet a reasonable measure in strength. If I could win a lady at leap-frog, or by vaulting into my saddle with my armor on my back, under the correction of bragging be it spoken, I should quickly leap into a wife. Or if I might buffet for my love, or bound my horse for her favors, I could

lay on like a butcher and sit like a jack-an-apes, never
off. But, Kate, I cannot look greenly nor gasp out my
eloquence, nor I have no cunning in protestation: only
downright oaths, which I never use till urged, nor never
break for urging. If thou canst love a fellow of this
temper, Kate, whose face is not worth sun-burning, that
never looks in his glass for love of anything he sees
there, let thine eye be thy cook. I speak to thee plain
soldier: if thou canst love me for this, take me: if not,
to say to thee that I shall die, is true; but for thy love,
no: yet I love thee too. And while thou livest, dear
Kate, take a fellow of plain and uncoined constancy;
for he perforce must do thee right, because he hath not
the gift to woo in other places: for these fellows of infinite tongue, that can rhyme themselves into ladies'
favors, they do always reason themselves out again.
What! a speaker is but a prater; a rhyme is but a
ballad. A good leg will fall; a straight back will
stoop; a black beard will turn white; a curled pate
will grow bald; a fair face will wither; a full eye will
wax hollow: but a good heart, Kate, is the sun and the
moon; or rather the sun and not the moon; for it shines
bright and never changes, but keeps his course truly.
If thou would have such a one, take me; and take me,
take a soldier; take a soldier, take a king. And what
sayest thou then to my love? speak, my fair, and fairly,
I pray thee.

Kath—Is it possible dat I sould love de enemy of
France?

K. Hen—No; it is not possible you should love the
enemy of France, Kate: but, in loving me, you should
love the friend of France; for I love France so well
that I will not part with a village of it; I will have it

all mine; and, Kate, when France is mine and I am yours, then yours is France and you are mine.

Kath—I cannot tell vat is dat.

K. Hen—No, Kate? I will tell thee in French; which I am sure will hang upon my tongue like a new-married wife about her husband's neck, hardly to be shook off. Je quand sur le possession de France, et quand vous avez le possession de moi—let me see, what then? Saint Denis be my speed!—donc votre est France et vous êtes mienne. It is as easy for me, Kate, to conquer the kingdom as to speak so much more French; I shall never move thee in French, unless it be to laugh at me.

Kath—Sauf votre honneur, le François que vous par-lez, il est meilleur que l'Anglois lequel je parle.

K. Hen—No, faith, is 't not, Kate; but thy speaking of my tongue, and I thine, most truly-falsely, must needs be granted to be much at one. But, Kate, dost thou understand thus much English, canst thou love me?

Kath—I cannot tell.

K. Hen—Can any of your neighbors tell Kate? I'll ask them. Come, I know thou lovest me; and at night, when you come into your closet, you 'll question this gentlewoman about me; and I know, Kate, you will to her dispraise those parts in me that you love with your heart; but, good Kate, mock me mercifully; the rather, gentle princess, because I love thee cruelly. How answer you, la plus belle Katharine du monde, mon très cher et devin déesse?

Kath—Your majestee ave faussee French enough to deceive de most sage demoiselle dat is in France.

K. Hen—Now, fie upon my false French! By mine

honor, in true English, I love thee, Kate; by which honor I dare not swear thou lovest me; yet my blood begins to flatter me that thou dost, notwithstanding the poor and untempering effect of my visage. I was created with a stubborn outside, with an aspect of iron, that, when I come to woo ladies, I fright them. But, in faith, Kate, the elder I wax, the better I shall appear; my comfort is, that old age, that ill layer up of beauty, can do no more spoil upon my face: thou hast me, if thou hast me, at the worst; and thou shalt wear me, if thou wear me, better and better: and, therefore, tell me, most fair Katharine, will you have me? Put off your maiden blushes; avouch the thoughts of your heart with the looks of an empress; take me by the hand, and say 'Harry of England, I am thine;' which word thou shalt no sooner bless mine ear withal, but I will tell thee aloud, 'England is thine, Ireland is thine, France is thine, and Henry Plantagenet is thine;' who, though I speak it before his face, if he be not fellow with the best king, thou shalt find the best king of good fellows. Come, your answer in broken music; for thy voice is music and thy English broken; therefore, queen of all, Katharine, break thy mind to me in broken English; wilt thou have me?

Kath—Dat is as it sall please de roi mon père.

K. Hen—Nay, it will please him well, Kate; it shall please him, Kate.

Kath—Den it sall also content me.

K. Hen—Upon that I kiss your hand, and I call you my queen.

Kath—Laissez, mon seigneur, laissez, laissez.

K. Hen—Then I will kiss your lips, Kate.

Kath—Il n'est pas la coutume de France.

K. Hen—Madam my interpreter, what says she?

Alice—Dat it is not be de fashion pour les ladies of France—I cannot tell vat is baiser en Anglish.

K. Hen—To kiss.

Alice—Your majesty entendre bettre que moi.

K. Hen—It is not a fashion for the maids in France to kiss before they are married, would she say?

Alice—Oui, vraiment.

K. Hen—O Kate, nice customs curtsy to great kings. Dear Kate, you and I cannot be confined within the weak list of a country's fashion: we are the makers of manners, Kate; and the liberty that follows our places stops the mouth of all find-faults; as I will do yours, for upholding the nice fashion of your country in denying me a kiss; therefore, patiently and yielding. [*Kissing her.*] You have witchcraft in your lips, Kate? there is more eloquence in a sugar touch of them than in the tongues of the French council; and they should sooner persuade Harry of England than a general petition of monarchs.

SHAKSPEARE.

COMBAT BETWEEN FITZ JAMES AND RODERICK DHU.

SCENE I.

Enter FITZ-JAMES (*Kneeling, with a braid of hair in his hand, which he fixes on his breast as he speaks*).

Fitz-James—Poor Blanche! no more by Devon-side
Thou'lt search for him who bravely died
Defending thee, his new-made bride.

Thy blood poured out for me demands
A signal vengeance at my hands.
And though Red Murdock low does lie,
His rebel chieftain too must die.
By Him whose word is truth! I swear
No other favor will I wear,
Till this sad token I imbrue
In the best blood of Roderick Dhu!
But hark! what means yon faint halloo?
Like bloodhounds now they seek me out;
I hear the whistle and the shout.
Well, I can perish sword in hand!

 Roderick—Thy name and purpose! Saxon, stand!
 Fitz—A stranger.
 Rod— ——What dost thou require?
 Fitz—Rest and a guide, and food and fire;
My life's beset, my path is lost,
The gale has chilled my limbs with frost.
 Rod—Art thou a friend to Roderick?
 Fitz—No.
 Rod—Thou darest not call thyself his foe?
 Fitz—I dare! to him and all the band
He brings to aid his murderous hand!
 Rod—Bold words, brave youth; they surely lie
Who said thou camest a secret spy!
 Fitz—"They do, indeed! Come, Roderick Dhu,
And of his clan the boldest two,
And let me but till morning rest,
I write the falsehood on their crest."—
 Rod—Stranger, I am to Roderick Dhu
A clansman born, a kinsman true;
Each word against his honor spoke,
Demands of me avenging stroke;

Yet more, upon thy fate, 'tis said,
A mighty augury is laid.
It rests with me to wind my horn,
Thou art with numbers overborne ;
It rests with me here, brand to brand,
Worn as thou art, to bid thee stand :
But, not for clan, nor kindred's cause,
Will I depart from honor's laws ;
To assail a wearied man were shame,
And stranger is a holy name ;
Guidance and rest, and food and fire,
In vain he never must require.
Then rest thee here till dawn of day ;
Myself will guide thee on the way,
O'er stock and stone, through watch and ward,
Till past Clan-Alpine's utmost guard,
As far as Coilantogle's ford ;
From thence thy warrant is thy sword.
Fitz—I take thy courtesy as 'tis given!
And, though thy foe, will proudly share
Thy soldier's couch, thy soldier's fare.

SCENE II.

Enter RODERICK *and* FITZ-JAMES.

Rod—Now, stranger, say, why wandered you
Without a pass from Roderick Dhu.
Fitz—My safest pass, in danger tried,
Hangs on my belt here, by my side.
Perhaps I sought a greyhound strayed ;
Perhaps I sought a Highland maid.
Rod—But, stranger, if in peace you came,
Bewildered in the mountain game.

Whence the bold boast by which you show
Sir Roderick's vowed and mortal foe?
   Fitz—Warrior, but yester-morn I knew
Naught of thy chieftain, Roderick Dhu,
Save as an outlawed, ruthless man,
The head of a rebellious clan.
But now, I am by promise tied
To match me with this man of pride ;
Twice have I sought Clan-Alpine's glen
In peace ; but when I come again,
I come with banner, brand and bow.
As leader seeks his mortal foe.
For love-lorn swain in lady's bower
Ne'er panted for the appointed hour,
As I, until before me stand
This rebel chieftain and his band !
   Rod—Have, then, thy wish ! Thy rashness rue!
(*Blows a whistle, when warriors appear on all sides.*)
Those are Clan-Alpine's warriors true ;
And, Saxon, I am Roderick Dhu !
   Fitz—(*Drawing his sword.*)
Come one, come all, this rock shall fly
From its firm base, as soon as I.
   Rod—(*Waves his hand and the soldiers disappear.*)
Fear nought—nay, that I need not say—
But—doubt not aught from mine array.
Thou art my guest—I pledged my word
As far as Coilantogle ford :
Nor would I call a clansman's brand
For aid against one valiant hand,
Though on our strife lay every vale
Rent by the Saxon from the Gael.
So move we on ; I only meant

To show the reed on which you leant,
Deeming this path you might pursue
Without a pass from Roderick Dhu.

(*They walk around the platform until Roderick suddenly
stops, and, facing Fitz-James, says:—*)
"Bold Saxon! to his promise just,
Vich-Alpine has discharged his trust.
This murderous chief, this ruthless man,
This head of a rebellious clan,
Hath led thee safe, through watch and ward,
Far past Clan-Alpine's outmost guard.
Now, man to man, and steel to steel,
A chieftain's vengeance thou shalt feel.
See, here, all vantageless I stand,
Armed like thyself with single brand;
For this is Coilantogle ford,
And thou must keep thee with thy sword.

Fitz—Sir Roderick, I have ne'er delayed,
When foeman bade me draw my blade;
Nay, more, brave chief, I vowed thy death:
Yet sure thy fair and generous faith,
And my deep debt for life preserved,
A better meed have well deserved.
Can naught but blood our feud atone?
Are there no means?

Rod—No, stranger, none!
And here—to fire thy flagging zeal—
The Saxon cause rests on thy steel:
For thus spoke Fate, by prophet bred
Between the living and the dead:
" Who spills the foremost foeman's life,
His party conquers in the strife."

Fitz—Then, by my word, the riddle's read;
Seek yonder brake beneath the cliff;
There lies Red Murdock, stark and stiff.
Thus Fate has solved her prophecy;
Then yield to Fate and not to me.

Rod—Soars thy presumption, then, so high?
Because a wretched kern ye slew,
Homage to name to Roderick Dhu?
He yields not, he, to man nor Fate!
Thou add'st but fuel to my hate:
My clansman's blood demands revenge.
Not yet prepared? Ah, then, I change
My thought, and hold thy valor light
As that of some vain carpet-knight,
Who ill deserved my courteous care,
And whose best boast is but to wear
A braid of his fair lady's hair.

Fitz—I thank thee, Roderick, for that word!
It nerves my heart, it steels my sword;
For I have sworn this braid to stain
In the best blood that warms thy vein.
Now, truce, farewell! and, ruth, begone!
Yet think not that by thee alone,
Proud chief, can courtesy be shown:
Though not from copse or heath or cairn,
Start at my whistle clansmen stern,
Of this small horn one feeble blast
Would fearful odds against thee cast.
But fear not—doubt not—which thou wilt;
We try this quarrel hilt to hilt.

*(As the speakers assume the attitude of combat the curtain
should fall.)*

ARRANGED AS A DIALOGUE BY J. HUGHES.

THE RIVALS.

ACT III, SCENE I.

The North Parade.

Enter CAPTAIN ABSOLUTE, L.

Capt. A.—'Tis just as Fag told me, indeed!—Whimsi·
cal enough, 'faith! My father wants to force me to
marry the very girl I am plotting to run away with!
He must not know of my connection with her yet awhile.
He has too summary a method of proceeding in these
matters; however, I'll read my recantation instantly.
My conversion is something sudden, indeed; but I can
assure him, it is very sincere.—So, so, here he comes—
he looks plaguy gruff! [*Steps aside,* L.]

Enter SIR ANTHONY, R.

Sir A.—No—I'll die sooner than forgive him! Die,
did I say? I'll live these fifty years to plague him. At
our last meeting his impudence had almost put me out
of temper—an obstinate, passionate, self-willed boy!
Who can he take after? This is my return for getting
him before all his brothers and sisters! for putting him,
at twelve years old, into a marching regiment, and
allowing him fifty pounds a year, besides his pay, ever
since! But I have done with him—he's anybody's son
for me—I never will see him more—never—never--
never—never.

Capt. A.—Now for a penitential face!
[*Comes forward on the* L.]
Sir A.—Fellow, get out of my way! [*Crosses,* R.]
Capt. A.—Sir, you see a penitent before you?

Sir A. [*turning his back*]—I see an impudent scoun-drel behind me.

Capt. A.—A sincere penitent. I am come, sir, to ac-knowledge my error, and to submit entirely to your will.

Sir A.—What's that?

Capt. A.—I have been revolving, and reflecting, and considering on your past goodness, and kindness, and condescension to me.

Sir A.—Well, sir?

Capt. A.—I have been likewise weighing and balanc-ing what you were pleased to mention concerning duty, and obedience, and authority.

Sir A. [*turning round*]—Why, now you talk sense, absolute sense; I never heard anything more sensible in my life. Confound you, you shall be Jack again!

Capt. A.—I am happy in the appellation.

Sir A.—Why then, Jack, my dear Jack, I will now in-form you who the lady really is. Nothing but your pas-sion and violence, you silly fellow, prevented me telling you at first. Prepare, Jack, for wonder and rapture—prepare! What think you of Miss Lydia Languish?

Capt. A.—Languish! What, the Languishes of Wor-cestershire?

Sir A.—Worcestershire! No! Did you never meet Mrs. Malaprop, and her niece, Miss Languish, who came into our country just before you were last ordered to your regiment.

Capt. A.—Malaprop! Languish! I don't remember ever to have heard the name before. Yet, stay: I think I do recollect something. Languish—Languish! She squints, don't she? A little red-haired girl?

Sir A.—Squints! A red-haired girl! Zounds, no!

Capt. A.—Then I must have forgot: it can't be the same person.

13

Sir A.—Jack, Jack! what think you of blooming, love-breathing seventeen?

Capt. A.—As to that, sir, I am quite indifferent : if I can please you in the matter, 'tis all I desire.

Sir A.—Nay, but Jack, such eyes! such eyes! so innocently wild! so bashfully irresolute! Not a glance but speaks and kindles some thought of love! Then, Jack, her cheeks! her cheeks, Jack! so deeply blushing at the insinuations of her tell-tale eyes! Then, Jack, her lips! Oh, Jack, lips, smiling at their own discretion! and, if not smiling, more sweetly pouting—more lovely in sullenness! Then, Jack, her neck! Oh! Jack! Jack!

Capt. A.—And which is to be mine, sir : the niece, or the aunt?

Sir A.—Why, you unfeeling, insensible puppy, I despise you! When I was of your age, such a description would have made me fly like a rocket! The aunt, indeed! Odds life! when I ran away with your mother I would not have touched any thing old or ugly to gain an empire!

Capt. A.—Not to please your father, sir?

Sir A.—To please my father—zounds! not to please— Oh! my father? Oddso! yes, yes! if my father, indeed had desired—that's quite another matter. Though he wasn't the indulgent father that I am, Jack.

Capt. A.—I dare say not, sir.

Sir A.—But, Jack, you are not sorry to find your mistress is so beautiful?

Capt. A.—Sir, I repeat it, if I please you in this affair, 'tis all I desire. Not that I think a woman the worse for being handsome ; but, sir, if you please to recollect, you before hinted something about a hump or two, one eye and a few more graces of that kind. Now.

without being very nice, I own I should rather choose a wife of mine to have the usual number of limbs, and a limited quantity of back; and though one eye may be very agreeable, yet, as the prejudice has always run in favor of two, I would not wish to affect a singularity in that article.

Sir A.—What a phlegmatic sot it is? Why, sirrah, you are an anchorite! a vile, insensible stock! You a soldier! you're a walking block, fit only to dust the company's regimentals on! Odds life, I've a great mind to marry the girl myself!

Capt. A.—I am entirely at your disposal, sir; if you should think of addressing Miss Languish yourself, I suppose you would have me marry the aunt; or if you should change your mind, and take the old lady, 'tis the same to me—I'll marry the niece.

Sir A.—Upon my word, Jack, thou art either a very great hypocrite, or—but, come, I know your indifference on such a subject must be all a lie—I'm sure it must. Come, now, confound your demure face; come, confess, Jack you have been lying, ha'nt you? You have been playing the hypocrite, hey? I'll never forgive you, if you ha'nt been lying and playing the hypocrite.

Capt. A.—I am sorry, sir, that the respect and duty which I bear to you should be so mistaken.

Sir A.—Hang your respect and duty! But come along with me. [*Crosses to* L.] I'll write a note to Mrs. Malaprop, and you shall visit the lady directly. Her eyes shall be the Promethean torch to you—come along, I'll never forgive you, if you don't come back stark mad with rapture and impatience—if you don't, 'egad, I'll marry the girl myself!   [*Exeunt,* L.]

LOCHIEL'S WARNING.

WIZARD.—Lochiel! Lochiel! beware of the day
    When the Lowlands shall meet thee in battle array!
For a field of the dead rushes red on my sight,
And the clans of Culloden are scattered in fight:
They rally!—they bleed!—for their kingdom and crown:
Woe, woe to the riders that trample them down!
Proud Cumberland prances, insulting the slain,
And their hoof-beaten bosoms are trod to the plain.
But hark! through the fast-flashing lightning of war,
What steed to the desert flies frantic and far?
'T is thine, O Glanullin! whose bride shall await,
Like a love-lighted watch-fire, all night at the gate.
A steed comes at morning: no rider is there;
But its bridle is red with the sign of despair.
Weep Albin! to death and captivity led!
Oh, weep! but thy tears cannot number the dead:
For a merciless sword o'er Culloden shall wave,
Culloden! that reeks with the blood of the brave.
    Lochiel.—Go, preach to the coward, thou death-telling
        seer,
Or, if gory Culloden so dreadful appear,
Draw, dotard, around thy old wavering sight,
This mantle, to cover the phantoms of fright.
    Wizard.—Ha! laugh'st thou, Lochiel, my vision to
        scorn?
Proud bird of the mountain, thy plume shall be torn!
Say, rushed the bold eagle exultingly forth,
From his home in the dark-rolling clouds of the North?
Lo! the death-shot of foemen outspeeding, he rode
Companionless, bearing destruction abroad;
But down let him stoop from his havoc on high!
Ah! home let him speed—for the spoiler is nigh.

Why flames the far summit? Why shoot to the blast
Those embers, like stars from the firmament cast?
'T is the fire-shower of ruin, all dreadfully driven
From his eyry, that beacons the darkness of heaven.
Oh, crested Lochiel! the peerless in might,
Whose banners arise on the battlements' height
Heaven's fire is around thee, to blast and to burn;
Return to thy dwelling, all lonely!—return!
For the blackness of ashes shall mark where it stood,
And a wild mother scream o'er her famishing brood.

    Lochiel.—False Wizard, avaunt! I have marshaled
        my clan;
Their swords are a thousand, their bosoms are one!
They are true to the last of their blood and their breath,
And like reapers descend to the harvest of death.
Then welcome be Cumberland's steed to the shock!
Let him dash his proud foam like a wave on the rock!
But woe to his kindred, and woe to his cause,
When Albin her claymore indignantly draws;
When her bonneted chieftains to victory crowd,
Clanranald the dauntless, and Moray the proud,
All plaided and plumed in their tartan array—

    Wizard.—Lochiel! Lochiel! beware of the day!
For, dark and despairing, my sight I may seal,
But man cannot cover what God would reveal:
'T is the sunset of life gives me mystical lore,
And coming events cast their shadows before. .
I tell thee, Culloden's dread echoes shall ring
With the blood-hounds that bark for thy fugitive king.
Lo! anointed by heaven with vials of wrath,
Behold, where he flies on his desolate path!
Now, in darkness and billows, he sweeps from my sight:
Rise! rise! ye wild tempests, and cover his flight!

'T is finished.   Their thunders are hushed on the moors:
Culloden is lost, and my country deplores:
But where is the iron-bound prisoner? where?
For the red eye of battle is shut in despair.
Say, mounts he the ocean-wave, banished, forlorn,
Like a limb from his country, cast bleeding and torn?
Ah, no! for a darker departure is near;
The war-drum is muffled; and black is the bier;
His death-bell is tolling; oh! mercy, dispel
You sight that it freezes my spirit to tell!
Life flutters, convulsed, in his quivering limbs,
And his blood-streaming nostril in agony swims.
Accursed be the fagots that blaze at his feet,
Where his heart shall be thrown, ere it ceases to beat,
With the smoke of its ashes to poison the gale—
    Lochiel.—Down, soothless insulter! I trust not the
    tale,
For never shall Albin a destiny meet,
So black with dishonor, so foul with retreat.
Though my perishing ranks should be strewed in their
    gore,
Like ocean-weeds heaped on the surf-beaten shore,
Lochiel, untainted by flight or by chains,
While the kindling of life in his bosom remains,
Shall victor exult, or in death be laid low,
With his back to the field and his feet to the foe,
And leaving in battle no blot on his name,
Look proudly to heaven from the death-bed of fame.

                                        CAMPBELL.

FROM THE TRAGEDY OF HAMLET.

ACT III, SCENE IV.

———

[Enter HAMLET.]

HAMLET—Now, mother, what's the matter?

Queen—Hamlet, thou hast thy father much offended.

Hamlet—Mother, you have my father much offended.

Queen—Come, come, you answer with an idle tongue.

Hamlet—Go, go, you question with a wicked tongue.

Queen—Why, how now, Hamlet!

Hamlet—What's the matter now?

Queen—Have you forgot me?

Hamlet—No, by the rood, not so.

You are the queen, your husband's brother's wife;

And—would it were not so!—you are my mother.

Queen— Nay, then, I'll set those to you that can speak.

Hamlet—Come, come, and sit you down; you shall not budge:

You go not till I set you up a glass

Where you may see the inmost part of you.

Queen—What wilt thou do? thou wilt not murther me?

Help, help, ho!

Polonius—[*Behind*] What, ho! help, help, help!

Hamlet—[*Drawing*] How now! a rat? Dead, for a
  ducat, dead! [*Makes a pass through the arras.*]

Polonius—[*Behind*] O, I am slain! [*Falls and dies.*]

Queen—O me, what hast thou done?

Hamlet—Nay, I know not;

Is it the king?

Queen—O, what a rash and bloody deed is this!

Hamlet—A bloody deed! almost as bad, good mother,

As kill a king, and marry with his brother.

Queen—As kill a king!

Hamlet—Ay, lady, 'twas my word.—

        [*Lifts up the arras and discovers Polonius.*]

Thou wretched, rash, intruding fool, farewell!

I took thee for thy better :

Leave wringing of your hands : peace! sit you down,

And let me wring your heart; for so I shall,

If it be made of penetrable stuff,

If damned custom have not braz'd it so

That it is proof and bulwark against sense.

Queen—What have I done, that thou darest wag thy
  tongue

In noise so rude against me?

Hamlet—Such an act

That blurs the grace and blush of modesty,

Calls virtue hypocrite, takes off the rose

From the fair forehead of an innocent love

And sets a blister there, makes marriage-vows

As false as dicers' oaths; O, such a deed

As from the body of contraction plucks

The very soul, and sweet religion makes

A rhapsody of words : heaven's face doth glow,

Yea, this sondity and compound mass,
With tristful visage, as against the doom,
Is thought-sick at the act.

    Queen—Ay me, what act,
That roars so loud and thunders in the index?

    Hamlet—Look here, upon this picture, and on this,
The counterfeit presentment of two brothers.
See, what a grace was seated on this brow;
Hyperion's curls; the front of Jove himself;
An eye like Mars, to threaten and command;
A station like the herald Mercury
New-lighted on a heaven-kissing hill;
A combination and a form indeed,
Where every god did seem to set his seal,
To give the world assurance of a man.
This was your husband. Look you now, what follows:
Here is your husband; like a mildew'd ear,
Blasting his wholesome brother. Have you eyes?
Could you on this fair mountain leave to feed,
And batten on this moor? Ha! have you eyes?
You cannot call it love, for at your age
The hey-day in the blood is tame, it's humble,
And waits upon the judgment; and what judgment
Would step from this to this?
O shame! where is thy blush?

    Queen—O Hamlet, speak no more;
Thou turn'st mine eyes into my very soul,
And there I see such black and grainèd spots
As will not leave their tinct.
O, speak to me no more;
These words like daggers enter in mine ears:
No more, sweet Hamlet!

    Hamlet—A murtherer and a villain;

A slave that is not twentieth part the tithe
Of your precedent lord; a vice of kings;
A cutpurse of the empire and the rule,
That from a shelf the precious diadem stole,
And put it in his pocket!
   Queen—No more!
   Hamlet—A king of shreds and patches,—

                            [*Enter* GHOST.]

Save me, and hover o'er me with your wings,
You heavenly guards!—What would your gracious
   figure?
   Queen—Alas! he's mad!
   Hamlet—Do you not come your tardy son to chide,
That, laps'd in time and passion, lets go by
The important acting of your dread command?
O, say!
   Ghost—Do not forget. This visitation
Is but to whet thy almost blunted purpose.
But, look, amazement on thy mother sits:
O, step between her and her fighting soul;
Speak to her Hamlet.
   Hamlet—How is it with you, lady?
   Queen—Alas, how is't with you,
That you do bend your eye on vacancy
And with the incorporal air do hold discourse?
                       O gentle son,
Upon the heat and flame of thy distemper
Sprinkle cool patience. Whereon do you look?
   Hamlet—On him, on him! Look you, how pale he
   glares!
His form and cause conjoin'd, preaching to stones,
Would make them capable. Do not look upon me;
Lest with this piteous action you convert

My stern effects; then what I have to do
Will want true color; tears perchance for blood.
   Queen—To whom do you speak this?
   Hamlet—Do you see nothing there?
   Queen—Nothing at all; yet all that is I see.
   Hamlet—Nor did you nothing hear?
   Queen—No, nothing but ourselves.
   Hamlet—Why, look you there! look, how it steals
     away!
My father, in his habit as he liv'd!
Look, where he goes, even now, out at the portal!
                         [*Exit Ghost.*]
   Queen—This is the very coinage of your brain;
This bodiless creation ecstasy
Is very cunning in.
   Hamlet—Ecstasy!
My pulse, as yours, doth temperately keep time,
And makes as healthful music: it is not madness
That I have utter'd; bring me to the test,
And I the matter will re-word, which madness
Would gambol from. Mother, for love of grace,
Lay not that flattering unction to your soul,
That not your trespass but my madness speaks;
It will but skin and film the ulcerous place,
Whilst rank corruption, mining all within,
Infects unseen. Confess yourself to heaven;
Repent what's past, avoid what is to come.
   Queen—O Hamlet, thou hast cleft my heart in
     twain.
   Hamlet—O, throw away the worser part of it,
And live the purer with the other half.
     For this same lord,   [*Pointing to Polonius.*]
I do repent;

I will bestow him, and will answer well
The death I gave him—So, again, good night.
I must be cruel, only to be kind ;
Thus bad begins, and worse remains behind.

SHAKSPEARE.

QUEEN MARY.

ACT V. SCENE V.

*London. A room in the palace. Mary. Lady Clarence.
Lady Magdalen Dacres. Alice. Queen pacing
the gallery. A writing-table in front. Queen
comes to the table and writes, and goes
again, still pacing the gallery.*

Lady Clarence—Mine eyes are dim; what hath she
written? Read.
Alice—" I am dying, Philip. Come to me."
Lady Magdalen—There, up and down, poor lady, up
and down.
Alice—And how her shadow crosses, one by one,
The moonlight casements pattern'd on the wall,
Following her like her sorrow. She turns again.
                    [*Queen sits and writes and goes again.*]
Lady Clarence—What hath she written now?
Alice—Nothing but "Come, come, come," and all
awry,
And blotted by her tears. This cannot last.
                              [*Queen returns.*]
Mary—I whistle to the bird has broken cage,
And all in vain. [*Sitting down.*]
Calais gone. Guisnes gone, too—and Philip's gone!

Lady Clarence—Dear madam, Philip is but at the
    wars ;
I cannot doubt but that he comes again;
And he is with you in a measure still.
I never looked upon so fair a likeness
As your great king in armor there,
His hand upon his helmet.
                [*Pointing to the portrait of Philip on the wall.*]
Mary—Doth he not look noble?
I had heard of him in battle over seas,
And I would have my warrior all in arms.
He said it was not courtly to stand helmeted
Before the Queen.   He had his gracious moments,
Altho' you'll not believe me.   How he smiles,
As if he loved me yet!
    Lady Clarence—And so he does.
    Mary—He never loved me—nay, he could not love
        me.
It was his father's policy against France.
I am eleven years older than he, poor boy.   [*Weeps.*]
    Alice [*aside*]—That was a lusty boy of twenty-seven
Poor enough in God's grace!
    Mary—And all in vain!
The Queen of Scots is married to the Dauphin,
And Charles the lord of this low world is gone,
And all his wars and wisdom pass'd away,
And in a moment I shall follow him.
    Lady Clarence—Nay, dearest lady, see your good
        physician.
    Mary—Drugs—but he knows they do not help me—
        says
That rest is all—tells me I must not think—
That I must rest.   I shall rest by and by.

Catch the wildcat, cage him, and when he
Springs and maims himself against the bars, say " rest !"
Why, you must kill him if you would have him rest.
Dead or alive you cannot make him happy.
    Lady Clarence—Your majesty has lived so pure a
      life,
And done such mighty things by Holy Church,
I trust that God will make you happy yet.
    Mary—What is this strange thing, happiness ?
Sit down here ;
Tell me thine happiest hour.
    Lady Clarence—I will, if that
Will make your grace forget yourself a little.
There runs a shallow brook across our field
For twenty miles, where the black crow flies **five,**
And doth so bound and babble all the way
As if itself were happy.   It was May-time,
And I was walking with the man I loved.
I loved him, but I thought I was not loved.
And both were silent, letting the wild brook
Speak for us—till he stoop'd and gather'd me
From out a bed of thick forget-me-nots,
Looked hard and sweet at me, and gave it me.
I took it, tho' I did not know I took it,
And put it in my bosom, and all at once
I felt his arms about me, and his lips—
    Mary—O ! God, I have been too slack, too slack.
There are Hot Gospellers even among our guards—
Nobles we dare not touch.   We have but burnt
The heretic priest, workmen, and women and children.
Wet, famine, ague, fever, storms, wreck, wrath,
We have so played the coward ; but by God's grace
We'll follow Philip's leading, and set up

The Holy Office here—garner the wheat,
And burn the tares with unquenchable fire !
Burn! Fire, what a savor! Tell the cooks to close
The doors of all the offices below. Latimer!
Sir, we are private with our women here—
Ever a rough, blunt and uncourtly fellow—
Thou light'st a torch that will never go out.
'Tis out—mine flames. Women, the Holy Father
Has ta'en the legateship from our Cousin Pole.
Was that well done? And poor Pole pines for it,
As I do, to the death. I am but a woman,
I have no power. Ah, weak and meek old man,
Seven-fold dishonor'd even in the sight
Of thine own sectaries—No, no. No pardon ı
Why, that was false! There is the right hand still
Beckons me hence.
Sir, you were burnt for heresy, not for treason,
Remember that! 'Twas I and Bonner did it,
And Pole. We are three to one. Have you found
      mercy there,
Grant it me here; and see he smiles and goes,
Gentle as in life.
      Alice—Madam, who goes? King Philip?
      Mary—No, Philip comes and goes, but never goes.
Women, when I am dead,
Open my heart, and there you'll find written
Two names, Philip and Calais. Open his—
So that he have one—
You will find Philip only, policy, policy—
Ay, worse than that—not one hour true to me!
Foul maggots crawling in a festered vice ı
Adulterous to the very heart of hell ı
Hast thou a knife?

Alice—Ay, madam, but o' God's mercy-
Mary—Fool, think'st thou I would peril mine own
    soul
By slaughter of the body? I could not, girl,
Not this way—callous with a constant stripe,
Unendurable. Thy knife!
    Alice—Take heed, take heed!
The blade is keen as death.
    Mary—This Philip shall not
Stare in upon me in my haggardness,
Old, miserable, diseased—
          Come thou down!
       [*Cuts out the picture and throws it down.*]
Lie there! [*Wails.*] O God, I have killed my Philip!
    Alice—No, madam; you have but cut the canvas
    out.
We can replace it.
    Mary—All is well, then; rest,
I will to rest; he said I must have rest.
       [*Cries of " Elizabeth " in the street.*]
A cry! What's that? Elizabeth? Revolt?
A new Northumberland? Another Wyatt?
I'll fight it out on the threshold of the grave.
    Lady Clarence—Madam, your royal sister comes to
    see you.
    Mary—I will not see her.
Who knows if Boleyn's daughter be my sister?
I will see none except the priest.
Your arm. [*To Lady Clarence.*]
O Saint of Aragon, with that sweet worn smile
Among thy patient wrinkles—
Help me hence. [*Exeunt.*]
                      TENNYSON.

COOL REASON.

EXTRACT FROM "THE RIVALS."

CHARACTERS.

FAG.	ACRES.
CAPTAIN ABSOLUTE.	SIR ANTHONY ABSOLUTE.

FAG—Sir, there is a gentleman below desires to see you—Shall I show him into the parlor?

Capt. Absolute—Ay—you may.

Acres—Well, I must be gone—

Capt. A.—Stay; who is it, Fag?

Fag—Your father, sir.

Capt. A.—You puppy, why did n't you show him up directly?   [*Exit* FAG.]

Acres—You have business with Sir Anthony.—I expect a message from Mrs. Malaprop, at my lodgings. I have sent also to my dear friend, Sir Lucius O'Trigger. —Adieu, Jack, we must meet at night, when you shall give me a dozen bumpers to little Lydia.   [*Exit.*]

Capt. A.—That I will, with all my heart. Now for a parental lecture—I hope he has heard nothing of the business that has brought me here—I wish the gout had held him fast in Devonshire, with all my soul!

Enter SIR ANTHONY.

Sir, I am delighted to see you here, and looking so well! —your sudden arrival at Bath made me apprehensive for your health.

Sir Anthony—Very apprehensive, I dare say, Jack.— What, you are recruiting here, hey?

Capt. A.—Yes, sir; I am on duty.

Sir A.—Well, Jack, I am glad to see you, though I did not expect it; for I was going to write to you on a little matter of business. Jack, I have been considering that I grow old and infirm, and shall probably not trouble you long.

Capt. A.—Pardon me, sir, I never saw you look more strong and hearty, and I pray fervently that you may continue so.

Sir A.—I hope your prayers may be heard, with all my heart. Now, Jack, I am sensible that the income of your commission, and what I have hitherto allowed you, is but a small pittance for a lad of your spirit.

Capt. A.—Sir, you are very good.

Sir A.—And it is my wish, while yet I live, to have my boy make some figure in the world.—I have resolved, therefore, to fix you at once in a noble independence.

Capt. A.—Sir, your kindness overpowers me.—Yet, sir, I presume you would not wish me to quit the army?

Sir A.—Oh! that shall be as your wife chooses.

Capt. A.—My wife, sir!

Sir A.—Ay, ay, settle that between you—settle that between you.

Capt. A.—A wife, sir, did you say?

Sir A.—Ay, a wife—why, did not I mention her before?

Capt. A.—Not a word of her, sir.

Sir A.—Odd so! I must n't forget her, though—Yes, Jack, the independence I was talking of, is by a marriage—the fortune is saddled with a wife—but I suppose that makes no difference?

Capt. A.—Sir! sir! you amaze me!

Sir A.—Why, what 's the matter with the fool? Just now you were all gratitude and duty.

Capt. A.—I was, sir,—you talked to me of independence and a fortune, but not a word of a wife.

Sir A.—Why—what difference does that make? Odds life, sir! if you have the estate, you must take it with the live stock on it, as it stands.

Capt. A.—Pray, sir, who is the lady?

Sir A.—What's that to you, sir?—Come, give me your promise to love, and to marry her directly.

Capt. A.—Sure, sir, this is not very reasonable, to summon my affections for a lady I know nothing of!

Sir A.—I am sure, sir, 'tis more unreasonable in you to object to a lady you know nothing of.

Capt. A.—You must excuse me, sir, if I tell you, once for all, that in this point I cannot obey you.

Sir A.—Harkye, Jack!—I have heard you for some time with patience—I have been cool—quite cool; but take care—you know I am compliance itself—when I am not thwarted; no one more easily led—when I have my own way;—but do n't put me in a frenzy.

Capt. A.—Sir, I must repeat it—in this, I cannot obey you.

Sir A.—Now, hang me if ever I call you Jack again while I live!

Capt. A.—Nay, sir, but hear me.

Sir A.—Sir, I won't hear a word—not a word! not one word! so give me your promise by a nod—and I'll tell you what, Jack—I mean, you dog—if you do n't—

Capt. A.—What, sir, promise to link myself to some mass of ugliness?

Sir A.—Zounds! Sirrah! the lady shall be as ugly as I choose: she shall have a hump on each shoulder; she shall be as crooked as the Crescent; her one eye shall roll like the bull's in Cox's Museum—she shall have a skin like a mummy, and the beard of a Jew—she shall be all this, sirrah!—yet I'll make you ogle her all day, and sit up all night to write sonnets on her beauty.

Capt. A.—This is reason and moderation indeed!

Sir A.—None of your sneering, puppy! no grinning, jackanapes!

Capt. A.—Indeed, sir. I never was in a worse humor for mirth in my life.

Sir A.—'T is false, sir; I know you are laughing in your sleeve; I know you 'll grin when I am gone, sirrah! *Capt. A.*—Sir, I hope I know my duty better.

Sir A.—None of your passion, sir! none of your violence, if you please—it won't do with me, I promise you. *Capt. A.*—Indeed, sir, I never was cooler in my life.

Sir A.—'T is a confounded lie!—I know you are in a passion in your heart; I know you are, you hypocritical young dog—but it won't do.

Capt. A.—Nay, sir, upon my word—

Sir A.—So, you will fly out! Can't you be cool, like me?—What good can passion do?—Passion is of no service, you impudent, insolent, overbearing reprobate!—There, you sneer again!—do n't provoke me! but you rely upon the mildness of my temper—you do, you dog! you play upon the meekness of my disposition! Yet take care—the patience of a saint may be overcome at last!—But mark!—I give you six hours and a half to consider of this: if you then agree, without any condition, to do everything on earth that I choose, why—confound you, I may in time forgive you—If not, zounds! do n't enter the same hemisphere with me! do n't dare to breathe the same air, or use the same light with me, but get an atmosphere and a sun of your own! I 'll strip you of your commission; I 'll lodge a five-and-threepence in the hands of trustees, and you shall live on the interest. I 'll disown you, I 'll disinherit you, I 'll unget you! and hang you if ever I call you Jack again! [*Exit.*]

Capt. A.—Mild, gentle, considerate father! I kiss your hands.—SHERIDAN.

MARY STUART.

From Schiller. *Act III., Scene II.*

CHARACTERS.

Mary—*Queen of Scotland.*	Robert—*Earl of Leicester.*
Elizabeth—*Queen of England.*	Talbot—*A friend of Mary.*

Enter Mary *and* Talbot.

MARY—Talbot, Elizabeth will soon be here. I cannot see her. Preserve me from this hateful interview.

Talbot—Reflect a while. Recall thy courage. The moment is come upon which everything depends. Incline thyself; submit to the necessity of the moment. She is the stronger. Thou must bend before her.

Mary—Before her? I cannot!

Tal.—Thou must do so. Speak to her humbly; invoke the greatness of her generous heart; dwell not too much upon thy rights. But see first how she bears herself towards thee. I myself did witness her emotion on reading thy letter. The tears stood in her eyes. Her heart, 't is sure, is not a stranger to compassion; therefore place more confidence in her, and prepare thyself for her reception.

Mary—(*Taking his hand*)—Thou wert ever my faithful friend. Oh, that I had always remained beneath thy kind guardianship, Talbot! Their care of me has indeed been harsh. Who attends her?

Tal.—Leicester. You need not fear him; the earl doth not seek thy fall. Behold, the queen approaches.

[*Retires.*]

Enter Elizabeth *and* Leicester.

Mary—(*Aside*)—O heavens! Protect me! her features say she has no heart!

Elizabeth—(To LEICESTER)—Who is this woman?
(*Feigning surprise.*) Robert, who has dared to—

Lei.—Be not angry, queen, and since heaven has
hither directed thee, suffer pity to triumph in thy noble
heart.

Tal.—(*Advancing*)—Deign, royal lady, to cast a look
of compassion on the unhappy woman who prostrates
herself at thy feet.

[MARY, *having attempted to approach* ELIZABETH, *stops
short, overcome by repugnance, her gestures indicating
internal struggle.*]

Eliz.—(*Haughtily*)—Sirs, which of you spoke of humility and submission? I see nothing but a proud lady,
whom misfortune has not succeeded in subduing.

Mary—(*Aside*)—I will undergo even this last degree
of ignominy. My soul discards its noble but, alas!
impotent pride. I will seek to forget who I am, what I
have suffered, and will humble myself before her who
has caused my disgrace. (*Turns to* ELIZABETH.)
Heaven, O sister, has declared itself on thy side, and
has graced thy happy head with the crown of victory.
(*Kneeling.*) I worship the Deity who hath rendered thee
so powerful. Show thyself noble in thy triumph, and
leave me not overwhelmed by shame! Open thy arms,
extend in mercy to me thy royal hand, and raise me
from my fearful fall.

Eliz.—(*Drawing back*)—Thy place, Stuart, is there,
and I shall ever raise my hands in gratitude to heaven
that it has not willed that I should kneel at thy feet, as
thou now crouchest in the dust at mine.

Mary—(*With great emotion*)—Think of the vicissitudes
of all things human! There is a Deity above who pun-
isheth pride. Respect the Providence who now doth

prostrate me at thy feet. Do not show thyself insensible and pitiless as the rock, to which the drowning man, with failing breath and outstretched arms, doth cling. My life, my entire destiny, depend upon my words and the power of my tears. Inspire my heart, teach me to move, to touch thine own. Thou turnest such icy looks upon me, that my soul doth sink within me, my grief parches my lips, and a cold shudder renders my entreaties mute. [*Rises.*]

Eliz.—(*Coldly*)—What wouldst thou say to me? thou didst seek converse with me. Forgetting that I am an outraged sovereign, I honor thee with my royal presence. 'Tis in obedience to a generous impulse that I incur the reproach of having sacrificed my dignity.

Mary—How can I express myself? how shall I so choose every word that it may penetrate, without irritating, thy heart? God of mercy! aid my lips, and banish from them whatever may offend my sister! I cannot relate to thee my woes without appearing to accuse thee, and this is not my wish. Towards me thou hast been neither merciful nor just. I am thine equal, and yet thou hast made me a prisoner, a suppliant, and a fugitive. I turned to thee for aid, and thou, trampling on the rights of nations and of hospitality, hast immured me in a living tomb! Thou hast abandoned me to the most shameful need, and finally exposed me to the ignominy of a trial! But, no more of the past; we are now face to face. Display the goodness of thy heart; tell me the crimes of which I am accused! Wherefore didst thou not grant me this friendly audience when I so eagerly desired it? Years of misery would have been spared me, and this painful interview would not have occurred in this abode of gloom and horror.

Eliz.—Accuse not fate, but thine own wayward soul

and the unreasonable ambition of thy house. There was
no quarrel between us until thy most worthy ally inspired
thee with the mad and rash desire to claim for thyself
the royal titles and my throne! Not satisfied with this,
he then urged thee to make war against me, to threaten
my crown and my life. Amidst the peace which reigned
in my dominions, he fraudulently excited my subjects to
revolt. But heaven doth protect me, and the attempt
was abandoned in despair. The blow was aimed at my
head, but 't is on thine that it will fall.

Mary—I am in the hand of my God, but thou wilt
not exceed thy power by committing a deed so atrocious?

Eliz.—What could prevent me? Thy kinsman has
shown monarchs how to make peace with their enemies!
Who would be surety for thee if, imprudently, I were to
release thee? How can I rely on thy pledged faith?
Nought but my power renders me secure. No! there
can be no friendship with a race of vipers.

Mary—Are these thy dark suspicions? To thine eyes,
then, I have ever seemed a stranger and an enemy. If
thou hadst but recognized me as heiress to thy throne—
as is my lawful right—love, friendship, would have made
me thy friend—thy sister.

Eliz.—What affection hast thou that is not feigned?
I declare thee heiress to my throne! Insidious treachery!
In order, forsooth, to overturn the state, and—wily
Armida that thou art—entrap within thy snares all the
youthful spirits of my kingdom, so that during my own
lifetime all eyes would turn towards thee—the new con-
stellation!

Mary—Reign on in peace! I renounce all right to thy
sceptre. The wings of my ambition have long drooped,
and greatness has no longer charms for me. 'T is thou
who hast it all; I am now only the shade of Mary

Stuart! My pristine ardor has been subdued by the ignominy of my chains. Thou hast nipped my existence
in the bud. But pronounce those magnanimous words
for which thou cam'st hither; for I will not believe that
thou art come to enjoy the base delight of insulting thy
victim! Pronounce the words so longed for, and say,
"Mary, thou art free! Till now thou hast known only
my power; now know my greatness." Woe to thee,
shouldst thou not depart from me propitious, beneficent,
like an invoked Deity. O sister! not for all England,
not for all the lands the vast ocean embraces, would I
present myself to thee with the inexorable aspect with
which thou now regardest me.

Eliz.—At length thou confessest thyself vanquished!
Hast thou emptied thy quiver of the artifices it con-
tained? Hast thou no more assassins? Does there not
remain to thee one single hero to undertake in thy de-
fence the duties of knight-errant? Gone, Mary, gone
forever are those days. Thou canst no longer seduce a
follower of mine; other causes now inflame men's
hearts. In vain didst thou seek a fourth husband among
my English subjects; they knew too well that thou mur-
derest thy husbands, as thou dost thy lovers.

Mary—(*Shuddering*)—O heavens! sister! Grant me
resignation.

Eliz.—(*To* LEICESTER, *with contempt*)—Earl, are these
the boasted features, on which no mortal eye could gaze
with safety? Is this the beauty to which no other
woman's could be compared? In sooth, the reputation
appears to have been easily won. To be thus celebrated
as the reigning beauty of the universe seems merely to
infer that she has been universal in the distribution of
her favors.

Mary—Ah, 't is too much!

Eliz.—(*With a smile of satisfaction*)—Now thou showest thyself in thine own form. Till now thou hast worn a mask.

Mary—(*With dignified pride*)—They were mere human errors that overcame my youth. My grandeur dazzled me. I have nought to conceal, nor deny my faults; my pride has ever disdained the base artifices of vile intriguers. The worst I ever did is known, and I may boast myself far better than my reputation. But woe to thee, thou malignant hypocrite, if thou ever lettest fall the mantle beneath which thou concealest thy shameless amours! Thou, the daughter of Anne Boleyn, hast not inherited virtue! The causes that brought thy sinful mother to the block are known to all.

Tal.—(*Stepping between them*)—Is this, O Mary, thine endurance? Is this thy humility?

Mary—Endurance? I have endured all that a mortal heart can bear. Hence, abject humility! Insulted patience, get ye from my heart! And thou, my long pent-up indignation, break thy bonds, and burst forth from thy lair! Oh, Thou gavest to the angry serpent his deadly glance ; arm my tongue with poisonous stings.

Tal.—(*To* ELIZABETH)—Forgive the angry transports which thou hast thyself provoked.

Lei.—(*Inducing* ELIZABETH *to withdraw*)—Hear not the ravings of a distracted woman. Leave this ill—

Mary—The throne of England is profaned by a base-born—the British nation is duped by a vile pretender! If right did prevail, thou wouldst be grovelling at my feet, for 't is I who am thy sovereign. (ELIZABETH *retires.* LEICESTER *and* TALBOT *follow.*) She departs, burning with rage, and with bitterness of death at heart. Now happy I am! I have degraded her in Leicester's presence. At last! at last! After long years of insult and contumely, I have at least enjoyed a season of triumph and revenge.—Adapted by J. HOWARD GORE.

SARACEN BROTHERS.

A TTENDANT—A stranger craves admittance to your
Highness.

Saladin—Whence comes he?

Attendant—That I know not.

Enveloped with a vestment of strange form,

His countenance is hidden; but his step,

His lofty port, his voice in vain disguised,

Proclaim,—if that I dare pronounce it,—

Saladin—Whom?

Attendant—Thy royal brother!

Saladin—Bring him instantly.   [*Exit attendant.*]

Now, with his specious, smooth, persuasive tongue,

Fraught with some wily subterfuge, he thinks

To dissipate my anger.   He shall die!

              [*Enter attendant and Malek Adhel.*]

Leave us together. [*Exit attendant.*] [*Aside.*] I should
know that form.

Now summon all thy fortitude, my soul,

Nor, though thy blood cry for him, spare the guilty!

[*Aloud.*]   Well, stranger, speak; but first unveil thyself,

For Saladin must view the form that fronts him.

Malek Adhel—Behold it, then!

Saladin—I see a traitor's visage.

Malek Adhel—A brother's!

Saladin—No!

Saladin owns no kindred with a villain.

Malek Adhel—O, patience, Heaven!   Had any tongue
but thine

Uttered that word, it ne'er should speak another.

Saladin—And why not now?   Can this heart be more
pierced

By Malek Adhel's sword than by his deeds?

O thou hast made a desert of this bosom!
For open candor, planted sly disguise;
For confidence, suspicion ; and the glow
Of generous friendship, tenderness and love,
Forever banished! Whither can I turn,
When he, by blood, by gratitude, by faith,
By every tie, bound to support, forsakes me?
Who, who can stand, when Malek Adhel falls?
Henceforth I turn me from the sweets of love,
The smiles of friendship; and this glorious world,
In which all find some heart to rest upon,
Shall be to Saladin a cheerless void,—
His brother has betrayed him!
    Malek Adhel—Thou art softened ;
I am thy brother, then ; but late thou saidst,—
My tongue can never utter the base title!
    Saladin—Was it traitor? True!   .
Thou hast betrayed me in my fondest hopes !
Villain? 'T is just; the title is appropriate!
Dissembler ? 'T is not written in thy face ;
No, nor imprinted on that specious brow;
But on this breaking heart the name is stamped,
Forever stamped with that of Malek Adhel!
Thinkest thou I'm softened ? By Mohammed! these hands
Should crush these aching eye-balls, ere a tear
Fall from them at thy fate! O monster, monster!
The brute that tears the infant from its nurse
Is excellent to thee ; for in his form
The impulse of his nature may be read ;
But thou, so beautiful, so proud, so noble,
O what a wretch art thou! O! can a term
In all the various tongues of man be found
To match thy infamy?

Malek Adhel—Go on! go on!
'Tis but a little time to hear thee, Saladin;
And, bursting at thy feet, this heart will prove
Its penitence, at least.

    Saladin—That were an end
Too noble for a traitor! The bowstring is
A more appropriate finish! Thou shalt die!

    Malek Adhel—And death were welcome at another's
      mandate!
What, what have I to live for? Be it so,
If that, in all thy armies, can be found
An executing hand.

    Saladin—O, doubt it not!
They 're eager for the office. Perfidy,
So black as thine, effaces from their minds
All memory of thy former excellence.

    Malek Adhel—Defer not, then, their wishes. Saladin,
If e'er this form was joyful to thy sight,
This voice seemed grateful to thine ear, accede
To my last prayer :—O, lengthen not this scene,
To which the agonies of death were pleasing!
Let me die speedily!

    Saladin—This very hour!
[*Aside*]—For, O, the more I look upon that face,
The more I hear the accents of that voice,
The monarch softens, and the judge is lost
In all the brother's weakness; yet such guilt,—
Such vile ingratitude,—it calls for vengeance;
And vengeance it shall have! What, ho! who waits there?
                       [*Enter attendant.*]

    Attendant—Did your highness call?

    Saladin—Assemble quickly
My forces in the court. Tell them they come
To view the death of yonder bosom traitor.

And, bid them mark, that he who will not spare
His brother when he errs, expects obedience,
Silent obedience, from his followers. [*Exit attendant.*]
Malek Adhel—Now, Saladin,
The word is given; I have nothing more
To fear from thee, my brother. I am not
About to crave a miserable life.
Without thy love, thy honor, thy esteem,
Life were a burden to me. Think not, either,
The justness of thy sentence I would question.
But one request now trembles on my tongue,
One wish still clinging round the heart; which soon
Not even that shall torture. Will it, then,
Thinkest thou, thy slumbers render quieter,
Thy waking thoughts more pleasing, to reflect,
That when thy voice had doomed a brother's death,
The last request which e'er was his to utter
Thy harshness made him carry to the grave?
    Saladin—Speak, then; but ask thyself if thou hast
    reason
To look for much indulgence here.
    Malek Adhel—I have not!
Yet will I ask for it. We part forever;
This is our last farewell; the king is satisfied;
The judge has spoke the irrevocable sentence.
None sees, none hears, save that Omniscient **Power,**
Which, trust me, will not frown to look upon
Two brothers part like such. When, in the face
Of forces once my own, I'm led to death,
Then be thine eye unmoistened; let thy voice
Then speak my doom untrembling; then,
Unmoved, behold this stiff and blackened corse.
But now I ask,—nay, turn not, Saladin!—
I ask one single pressure of thy hand;

From that stern eye, one solitary tear,—
O torturing recollection!—one kind word
From the loved tongue which once breathed naught but
    kindness.
Still silent? Brother! friend! beloved companion
Of all my youthful sports!—are they forgotten?—
Strike me with deafness, make me blind, O Heaven!
Let me not see this unforgiving man
Smile at my agonies! nor hear that voice
Pronounce my doom, which would not say one word,
One little word, whose cherished memory
Would soothe the struggles of departing life!
Yet, yet thou wilt! O, turn thee, Saladin!
Look on my face,—thou canst not spurn me then;
Look on the once-loved face of Malek Adhel
For the last time, and call him—
    Saladin—(*Seizing his hand*)—Brother! brother!
    Malek Adhel—(*Breaking away*)—Now call thy fol-
    lowers;
Death has not now
A single pang in store. Proceed! I'm ready.
    Saladin—O, art thou ready to forgive, my brother?
To pardon him who found one single error,
One little failing, 'mid a splendid throng
Of glorious qualities—
    Malek Adhel—O, stay thee, Saladin!
I did not ask for life—I only wished
To carry thy forgiveness to the grave.
No, Emperor, the loss of Cesarea
Cries loudly for the blood of Malek Adhel.
Thy soldiers, too, demand that he who lost
What cost them many a weary hour to gain,
Should expiate his offences with his life.

Lo! even now they crowd to view my death,
Thy just impartiality. I go,
Pleased by my fate to add one other leaf
To thy proud wreath of glory.   [*Going.*]
Saladin—Thou shalt not.   [*Enter attendant.*]
    Attendant—My lord, the troops assembled by your order
Tumultuous throng the courts. The prince's death
Not one of them but vows he will not suffer.
The mutes have fled; the very guards rebel.
Nor think I, in this city's spacious round,
Can e'er be found a hand to do the office.
    Malek Adhel—O faithful friends!—(*To attendant*)—
    Thine shalt.
    Attendant—Mine? Never!
The other first shall lop it from the body.
    Saladin—They teach the Emperor his duty well.
Tell them he thanks them for it. Tell them, too,
That ere their opposition reached our ears,
Saladin had forgiven Malek Adhel.
    Attendant—O joyful news!
I haste to gladden many a gallant heart,
And dry the tear on many a hardy cheek,
Unused to such a visitor.   [*Exit.*]
    Saladin—These men, the meanest in society,
The outcasts of the earth,—by war, by nature,
Hardened, and rendered callous,—these who claim
No kindred with thee,—who have never heard
The accents of affection from thy lips,—
O, these can cast aside their vowed allegiance,
Throw off their long obedience, risk their lives,
To save thee from destruction. While I,
I, who can not, in all my memory,
Call back one danger which thou hast not shared,
One day of grief, one night of revelry,
Which thy resistless kindness hath not soothed,

Or thy gay smile and converse rendered sweeter,—
I, who have thrice in the ensanguined field,
When death seemed certain, only uttered—" Brother! "
And seen that form, like lightning, rush between
Saladin and his foes, and that brave breast
Dauntless exposed to many a furious blow
Intended for my own,—I could forget
That 't was to thee I owed the very breath
Which sentenced thee to perish! O, 't is shameful!
Thou canst not pardon me!
　　Malek Adhel—By these tears, I can!
O brother! from this very hour, a new,
A glorious life commences! I am all thine!
Again the day of gladness or of anguish
Shall Malek Adhel share; and oft again
May this sword fence thee in the bloody field.
Henceforth, Saladin,
My heart, my soul, my sword, are thine forever!

THE BRIDAL WINE-CUP.

SCENE----*Parlor, with wedding party, consisting of Judge*
Otis; MARION, *his daughter, the bride;* HARRY
WOOD, *the bridegroom; a few relatives and friends;
all gathered around the center table, on which are decan-
ters and wine-glasses.*

ONE OF THE COMPANY—Let us drink the health
of the newly-wedded pair. (*Turns to Harry.*) Shall it
be in wine? (*turns to Marion,*) or in sparkling cold water?

　　Harry—Pledge in wine, if it be the choice of the company.

　　Several voices—Pledge in wine, to be sure.

　　Marion—(*With great earnestness.*)—O no! Harry; not
with wine, I pray you.

　　Judge Otis—Yes, Marion, my daughter; lay aside

your foolish prejudices for this once; the company expect
it, and you should not so seriously infringe upon the rules
of etiquette. In your own house you may act as you
please; but in mine, which you are about to leave, for
this once please me, by complying with my wishes in
this matter.

[*A glass of wine is handed to* MARION, *which she
slowly and reluctantly raises to her lips, but just
as it reaches them she exclaims, excitedly, holding
out the glass at arm's length, and staring at it,*]

Marion—Oh! how terrible!

Several voices—(*Eagerly*)—What is it? What do you
see?

Marion—Wait—wait, and I will tell you. I see
(*pointing to the glass with her finger*) a sight that beggars
all description ; and yet listen, and I will paint it for you,
if I can. It is a lonely spot; tall mountains, crowned
with verdure, rise in awful sublimity around; a river
runs through, and bright flowers in wild profusion grow
to the water's edge. There is a thick, warm mist, that
the sun vainly seeks to pierce ; trees, lofty and beautiful,
wave to the airy motion of the birds; and beneath them
a group of Indians gather. They move to and fro with
something like sorrow upon their dark brows; for in
their midst lies a manly form, whose cheek is deathly
pale, and whose eye is wild with the fitful fire of fever.
One of his own white race stands, or rather kneels, beside
him, pillowing the poor sufferer's head upon his breast
with all a brother's tenderness. Look! (*she speaks with
renewed energy,*) how he starts up, throws the damp curls
back from his high and noble brow, and clasps his hands
in agony of despair; hear his terrible shrieks for life ;
mark how he clutches at the form of his companion.

imploring to be saved from despair and death. O,
what a terrible scene! Genius in ruins, pleading for
that which can never be regained when once lost. Hear
him call piteously his father's name; see him clutch his
fingers as he shrieks for his sister—his only sister, the
twin of his soul—now weeping for him in his distant
home! See! his hands are lifted to heaven ; he prays—
how wildly!—for mercy, while the hot fever rushes
through his veins. The friend beside him is weeping in
despair; and the awe-stricken sons of the forest move
silently away, leaving the living and the dying alone
together. (*The judge, overcome with emotion, falls into
a chair, while the rest of the company seem awe-struck,
as Marion's voice grows softer and more sorrowful in its
tones, yet remains distinct and clear.*) It is evening now ;
the great, white moon is coming up, and her beams fall
gently upon his forehead. He moves not ; for his eyes
are set in their socket, and their once piercing glance is
dim. In vain his companion whispers the name of
father and sister; death is there to dull the pulse, to
dim the eye, and to deafen the ear. Death! stern, terrible, and with no soft hand, no gentle voice, to soothe his
fevered brow, and calm his troubled soul and bid it hope
in God. (*Harry sits down and covers his face with his
hands.*) Death overtook him thus; and there, in the
midst of the mountain forest, surrounded by Indian
tribes, they scooped him a grave in the sand ; and without a shroud or coffin, prayer or hymn, they laid him
down in the damp earth to his final slumber. Thus
died and was buried the only son of a proud father ; the
only, idolized brother of a fond sister.. There he sleeps
to-day, undisturbed, in that distant land, with no stone
to mark the spot. There he lies—*my father's son*—MY
OWN TWIN BROTHER! A victim to this (*holds up the*

glass before the company) deadly, damning poison!
Father! *(turning to the judge,)* father, shall I drink it
now?

*Judge Otis—(Raising his bowed head and speaking
with faltering voice)*—No, no, my child! in God's name,
cast it away.

Marion—(Letting her glass fall and dash to pieces)—
Let no friend who loves me hereafter tempt me to peril
my soul for wine. Not firmer the everlasting hills than
my resolve, God helping me, never to touch or taste that
terrible poison. And he, *(turning to Harry,)* to whom I
have this night given my heart and hand, who watched
over my brother's dying form in that last sad hour, and
buried the poor wanderer there by the river, in that land
of gold, will, I trust, sustain me in this resolve. Will
you not, *(offers him her hand, which he takes,)* my
husband?

Harry—With the blessing of Heaven upon my efforts,
I will; and I thank you, beyond expression, for the
solemn lesson you have taught us all on this occasion.

Judge Otis—God bless you, *(taking Marion and Harry
by the hand, and speaking with deep emotion,)* my children; and may I, too, have grace given me to help you
in your efforts to keep this noble resolve.

One of the company—Let us honor the firmness and
nobleness of principle of the fair bride, by drinking
her health in pure, sparkling water, the only beverage
which the great Creator of the Universe gave to the
newly-wedded pair in the beautiful Garden of Eden.

DRAMATIZED BY SIDNEY HERBERT.

PRINCE HENRY AND FALSTAFF.

KING HENRY IV., ACT II, SCENE IV.

———

PRINCE HENRY *and* POINS, *in a back room, in a tavern.*
Enter FALSTAFF, GADSHILL, BARDOLPH, *and* PETO.

POINS—Welcome, Jack. Where hast thou been?
Falstaff—A plague of all cowards, I say, and a
vengeance too! marry and amen! Give me a cup of
sack, boy. Ere I lead this life long, I'll sew nether‑
socks, and mend them, and foot them too. A plague of
all cowards! Give me a cup of sack, rogue. Is there
no virtue extant? [*He drinks, and then continues.*] You
rogue, here's lime in this sack: there's nothing but
roguery to be found in villanous man: yet a coward is
worse than a cup of sack, with lime in it; a villanous
coward. Go thy ways, old Jack; die when thou wilt: if
manhood, good manhood, be not forgot upon the face of
the earth, then am I a shotten herring. There live not
three good men unhanged, in England; and one of them
is fat and grows old; a bad world, I say! I would I
were a weaver; I could sing psalms, or any thing; a
plague of all cowards, I say still.
Prince Henry—How now, wool-sack? What mutter
you?
Fal.—Thou art a king's son. Now, if I do not beat
thee out of thy kingdom with a dagger of lath, and drive

all thy subjects afore thee like a flock of wild geese, I'll never wear hair on my face more. You prince of Wales!

P. Henry—Why, you base-born dog! What's the matter?

Fal.—Are you not a coward? Answer me to that; and Poins there?

Poins—Zounds, ye fat paunch, an ye call me coward, I'll stab thee.

Fal.—I call thee coward? I'll see thee hanged ere I call thee coward: but I would give a thousand pounds I could run as fast as thou canst. You are straight enough in the shoulders, you care not who sees your back: call you that backing of your friends? A plague upon such backing! Give me them that will face me. Give me a cup of sack. I am rogue, if I have drunk to-day.

P. Henry—O villain! thy lips are scarce wiped, since thou drank'st last.

Fal.—All's one for that. A plague of all cowards, still say I.

P. Henry—What's the matter?

Fal—What's the matter! There be four of us here have ta'en a thousand pounds this morning.

P. Henry—Where is it, Jack? Where is it?

Fal.—Where is it? Taken from us it is; a hundred upon poor four of us.

P. Henry—What! a hundred, man?

Fal.—I am a rogue, if I were not at half sword with a dozen of them, for two hours together. I have 'scaped by miracle. I am eight times thrust through the doublet; four, through the hose; my buckler cut through and through; my sword hacked like a hand-saw; look here: [*shows his sword*]. I never dealt better since I was a man; all would not do. A plague of all cowards! Let them speak [*pointing to* GADSHILL, BARDOLPH *and*, PETO];

if they speak more or less than truth, they are villains and the sons of darkness.

P. Henry—Speak, sirs; how was it?

Gadshill—We four set upon some dozen—

Fal.—Sixteen, at least, my lord.

Gad.—And bound them.

Peto—No, no, they were not bound.

Fal.—You rogue, they were bound, every man of them · ɵr I am a Jew, else—an Ebrew Jew.

Gad.—As we were sharing, some six or seven fresh men set upon us—

Fal.—And unbound the rest; and then come in the other.

P. Henry—What! fought ye with them all?

Fal.—All? I know not what ye call all; but if I fought not with fifty of them, I am a bunch of radish: if there were not two or three and fifty upon poor old Jack, then I am no two-legged creature.

P. Henry—Pray heaven, you have not murdered some of them.

Fal.—Nay, that's past praying for; for I have pep-pered two of them; two I am sure I have paid; two rogues in buckram suits. I tell thee what, Hal, if I tell thee a lie, spit in my face, and call me a horse. Thou knowest my old ward [*he draws his sword, and stands as if about to fight*]; here I lay, and thus I bore my point. Four rogues in buckram let drive at me—

P. Henry—What! four? Thou saidst but two even now.

Fal.—Four, Hal; I told thee four.

Poins—Ay, ay, he said four.

Fal.—These four came all a-front, and mainly thrust at me. I made no more ado, but took all their seven points on my target, thus.

P. Henry—Seven? Why, there were but four, even now.

Fal.—In buckram?

Poins—Ay, four in buckram suits.

Fal.—Seven, by these hilts, or I am a villain else.

P. Henry—Pr'ythee, let him alone, we shall have more anon.

Fal.—Dost thou hear me, Hal?

P. Henry—Ay, and mark thee, too, Jack.

Fal.—Do so, for it is worth the listening to. These nine men in buckram, that I told thee of—

P. Henry—So, two more already.

Fal.—Their points being broken, began to give me ground; but I followed me close, came in foot and hand; and, with a thought, seven of the eleven I paid.

P. Henry—O, monstrous! eleven buckram men grown out of two!

Fal.—But three knaves, in Kendal green, came at my back, and let drive at me; for it was so dark, Hal, that thou couldst not see thy hand.

P. Henry—These lies are like the father of them; gross as a mountain, open, palpable. Why, thou clay-brained, thou knotty-pated fool; thou greasy tallow-keech—

Fal.—What! Art thou mad? Art thou mad? Is not the truth the truth?

P. Henry—Why, how couldst thou know these men in Kendal green, when it was so dark thou couldst not see thy hand? Come, tell us your reason; What sayst thou to this?

Poins—Come, your reason, Jack; your reason.

Fal.—What, upon compulsion? No, were I at the strappado, or all the racks in the world, I would not tell you on compulsion. Give you a reason on compulsion? If reasons were as plenty as blackberries, I would give no man a reason on compulsion.

P. Henry—I'll no longer be guilty of this sin : this sanguine coward, this bed-presser, this horse-back-breaker, this huge hill of flesh—

Fal.—Away! you starveling, you eel-skin, you dried neat's tongue, you stock-fish—O for breath to utter what is like thee!—you tailor's yard, you sheath, you bow-case, you—

P. Henry—Well, breathe a while, and then to 't again ; and when thou hast tired thyself in base comparisons, hear me speak but this.

Poins—Mark, Jack.

P. Henry—We two, saw you four, set on four ; you bound them, and were masters of their wealth. Mark now, how plain a tale shall put you down. Then did we two, set on you four, and with a word out-faced you from your prize, and have it ; yea, and can show it to you, here in the house : and, Falstaff, you carried yourself away as nimbly, with as quick dexterity, and roared for mercy, and still ran and roared, as ever I heard a calf. What a slave art thou, to hack thy sword as thou hast done, and then say it was in fight. What trick, what device, what starting-hole canst thou now find out to hide thee from this open and apparent shame?

Poins—Come, let 's hear, Jack. What trick hast thou now?

Fal.—Why, I knew ye, as well as he that made ye. Why, hear ye, my masters : was it for me to kill the heir-apparent? Should I turn upon the true prince? Why, thou knowest, I am as valiant as Hercules ; but beware instinct ; the lion will not touch the true prince ; instinct is a great matter ; I was a coward on instinct. I shall think the better of myself and thee, during my life ; I for a valiant lion, and thou for a true prince. But, lads, I am glad you have the money. Hostess, clap to the doors.

Watch to-night, pray to-morrow. Gallants, lads, boys, hearts of gold ; all the titles of good fellowship come to you! What, shall we be merry? Shall we have a play extempore?

P. Henry—Content; and the argument shall be thy running away.

Fal.—Ah! no more of that, Hal, an thou lovest me.

SHAKESPEARE.

PARTHENIA.

The father of the beautiful Greek maiden, PARTHENIA, *was taken prisoner by the barbarous* ALEMANNI. *She leaves her home and goes to the mountains to accomplish his rescue; she succeeds in persuading the barbarian chief,* INGOMAR, *to take her as hostage, and allow him to return home and work for her ransom. She promises that she will work for them, and never give way to woman's weakness. The following is a scene succeeding the departure of* MYROM, *the father of* PARTHENIA.

PARTHENIA *stands with hands before her face, sobbing.* INGOMAR *comes forward.*

INGOMAR—Ha! do I see right?—You weep! Is that the happy temper that you boast?

Parthenia—Oh, I shall never see him more!

Ing.—What! have we for a silly old man got now a foolish, timid, weeping girl? I have had enough of tears.

Par.—Enough, indeed, since you but mock them. 1 will not—no! I'll weep no more!

[*She dries her eyes and retires to the background.*]

Ing.—That's good ;—come, that looks well. She is a

brave girl!—she rules herself, and, if she keep her word,
we have made a good exchange. I'll weep no more!—
aha! I like the girl, and if—Ho! whither goest thou?

[*To* PARTHENIA, *who is going off with two goblets.*]

Par.—Where should I go?—to yonder brook to cleanse
the cups.

Ing.—No! stay and talk to me.

Par.—I have duties to perform.   [*Going.*]

Ing.—Stay—I command you, slave!

Par.—I am no slave!—your hostage, but no slave. I
go to cleanse the cups.   [*Exit.*]

Ing.—Ho! here's a self-willed thing—here's a spirit!
(*mimicking her*). I will not, I am no slave! I have
duties to perform! Take me for hostage! and she flung
back her head, as though she brought with her a ton of
gold. I'll weep no more!—aha! an impudent thing;
she pleases me! I love to be opposed; I love my horse
when he rears, my dogs when they snarl; the mountain-
torrent, and the sea when it flings its foam up to the
stars;—such things as this fill me with life and joy.
Tame indolence is living death!—the battle of the strong
alone is life!

PARTHENIA *returns with the cups and a bunch of field-*
flowers; she seats herself on a rock. INGOMAR *approaches*
her.

Ing.—Ah! she is here again. What art thou making
there?

Par.—I?—garlands.

Ing.—Garlands?—(*Aside*)—It seems to me as I had
seen her before in a dream! How is it?—Ah! my
brother!—he who died a child—yes, that is it—my little
Folko. She has his dark brown hair, his sparkling eye:
even the voice seems known to me again. I'll not to

sleep, I'll talk to her:—(*To Parthenia*)—These you call garlands, and wherefore do you weave them?

Par.—For these cups.

Ing.—How?

Par.—Is it not with you a custom? With us, at home, we love to intertwine with flowers our cups and goblets.

Ing.—What use is such a plaything?

Par.—Use? they are beautiful; that is their use. The sight of them makes glad the eye; their scent refreshes, cheers. There, is not that beautiful?

[*She fastens the half-finished garland round a cup, and presents it to him.*]

Ing.—Ay—by the bright sun! That dark green mixed up with the gay flowers! Thou must teach our women to weave such garlands.

Par.—That is soon done: thy wife herself shall soon weave wreaths as well as I.

Ing.—(*Laughing*)—My wife! my wife! a woman, dost thou say? I thank the gods not I. This is my wife—(*points to his arms*)—my spear, my sword, my shield; let him who will waste cattle, slaves, or gold, to buy a woman—not I—not I!

Par.—To buy a woman! how? Did I hear aright? bargain for brides as you would slaves—buy them like cattle?

Ing.—Well, I think a woman fit only for a slave. We follow our customs as you yours. How do you in your city there?

Par.—Consult our hearts. Massilia's free-born daughters are not sold, but bound by choice with bands as light and sweet as these I hold. Love only buys us there.

Ing.—Marry for love—that's strange! I cannot comprehend. I love my horse, my dogs, my brave companions, but no woman! What dost thou mean by love?—what is it, girl?

Par.—What is it? 'T is of all things the most sweet— the heaven of life—or so my mother says: I never felt it.

Ing.—Never?

Par.—No, indeed. Now look: this garland—how beautiful! Here would I weave red flowers if I had them.

Ing.—Yonder, there, in that thick wood they grow.

Par.—There, sayest thou?· Oh, what a lovely red! go pluck me some!

Ing.—I go for thee!—the master for the slave! and yet, why not? I'll go! the poor child's tired.

Par.—Dost thou hesitate?

Ing.—No; thou shalt have the flowers, as fresh and dewy as the bush affords. [*He goes off.*]

Par.—I never succeeded half so well; it will be charming! Charming? and for whom? Here among savages! No mother here looks smiling on it. I am alone, forsaken! But no, I'll weep no more!—no, none shall say I fear.

INGOMAR *enters with a bunch of flowers.*

Ing.—There are the flowers.

Par.—Thanks! thanks! Oh, thou hast broken them too short off in the stem.

[*She throws some of them on the ground.*]

Ing.—Shall I get thee more?

Par.—No; these will do.

Ing.—Tell me now about your home. I will sit here near thee.

Par.—Not there! thou art crushing all my flowers!

Ing.—(*Seats himself at her feet*)—Well, well; I will sit here then, and now tell me, what is thy name?

Par.—Parthenia.

Ing.—Parthenia! a pretty name! And now, Parthenia, tell me which you call love grows in the soul, and what love is. 'T is strange, but in that word seems something fathomless like yonder ocean.

Par.—How shall I say! Love comes, my mother says, like flowers in the night—reach me those violets;—it is a flame a single look will kindle, but not an ocean quench. Fostered by dreams, excited by each thought, love is a star from heaven, that points the way and leads us to its home—a little spot in Earth's dry desert, where the soul may rest—a grain of gold in the dull sand of life—a foretaste of Elysium; but when, weary of this world's woes, the immortal gods flew to the skies, with all their richest gifts, love stayed behind, self-exiled for man's sake.

Ing.—I never heard aught so beautiful!—but still I comprehend it not.

Par.—Nor I, for I have never felt it; yet I know a song my mother sung, that plainly speaks of love, at least to me. How goes it? stay!

[*Sings slowly, as if trying to recollect.*]

What love is, if thou wouldst be taught,
    Thy heart must teach alone—
Two souls with but a single thought,
    Two hearts that beat as one.

And whence comes love?—like morning's light
    It comes without thy call;
And how dies love?—a spirit bright,
    Love never dies at all.

And when—and when—

Ing.—Go on!
Par.—I know no more.

Ing.—(*Impatiently*)—Try!—try!

Par.—I cannot now; but at some other time I may remember.

Ing.—(*Authoritatively*)—Now! Go on, I say!

Par.—(*Springing up*)—Not now; I want more roses for my wreath!—yonder they grow; I will fetch them for myself. Take care of all my flowers and the wreath!

[*Runs off.*]

Ing.—(*In deep abstraction*)—

Two souls with but a single thought,
Two hearts that beat as one.

TRANSLATION FROM THE GERMAN.

TRIAL SCENE.

From " Merchant of Venice," in which the following characters are introduced.

DUKE OF VENICE.	PORTIA, *the wife of Bassanio.*
ANTONIO, *a merchant.*	SHYLOCK, *a Jew.*
BASSANIO, *his intimate friend.*	GRATIANO, *the enemy of the Jew.*

The merchant Antonio had borrowed for his friend Bassanio, from Shylock, the Jew, the sum of 3000 ducats; and Shylock had caused to be inserted in the bond, the condition, that if Antonio should fail to make payment on a certain day, he should forfeit a pound of flesh to be cut off nearest his heart.

Owing to losses, Antonio was unable to pay on the day appointed: and although his friends afterwards offered to make double, treble and even quadruple payment to the Jew, the latter claimed, as he had a right, by the strict "law of Venice," exact fulfilment of the bond. In this scene Portia, the wife of Bassanio, a lady of high mental powers and great goodness, but here so disguised as a learned doctor and judge from Padua, as to be unrecognized even by her own husband, is introduced to counsel with the Duke in the administration of justice.

The parties appear in court before the Duke of Venice.

DUKE—Give me your hand. Came you from old Bellario?

Portia—I did, my lord.

Duke—You are welcome: take your place.
Are you acquainted with the difference
That holds this present question in the court?

Portia—I am informed thoroughly of the cause.
Which is the merchant here, and which the Jew?
Duke—Antonio and old Shylock, both stand forth.
Portia—Is your name Shylock?
Shylock—Shylock is my name.
Portia—Of a strange nature is the suit you follow;
Yet in such rule, that the Venetian law
Can not impugn you as you do proceed.
You stand within his danger, do you not? (*To Antonio.*)
Antonio—Ay, so he says.
Portia—Do you confess the bond?
Antonio—I do.
Portia—Then must the Jew be merciful.
Shylock—On what *compulsion* must I? tell me that.
Portia—The quality of mercy is not strained;
It droppeth as the gentle rain from heaven
Upon the place beneath; it is twice blessed;
It blesseth him that gives, and him that takes.
'T is mightiest in the mightiest. It becomes
The throned monarch better than his crown:
His *scepter* shows the force of *temporal* power,
The attribute to awe and majesty,
Wherein doth sit the dread and fear of kings:
But *mercy* is above this sceptered sway;
It is enthroned in the hearts of kings;
It is an attribute to God himself;
And earthly power doth then show likest God's
When mercy seasons justice. Therefore, Jew,
Though justice be thy plea, consider this—
That, in the course of justice, none of us
Should see salvation: we do *pray* for mercy;
And that same prayer doth teach us all to render
The deeds of mercy. I have spoke thus much
To mitigate the justice of thy plea;

Which if thou follow, this strict court of Venice
Must needs give sentence 'gainst the merchant there.

Shylock—My deeds upon my head! I crave the *law*,
The penalty and forfeit of my *bond*.

Portia—Is he not able to discharge the money?

Bassanio—Yes, here I tender it for him in the court;
Yea, *twice* the sum; if that will not suffice,
I will be bound to pay it ten times o'er,
On forfeit of my hands, my head, my heart:
If this will not suffice, it must appear
That malice bears down truth. And I beseech **you,**
Wrest once the law to your authority:
To do a *great right*, do a *little wrong*,
And curb this cruel devil of his will.

Portia—It must not be; there's no power in Venice
Can alter a decree established;
'T will be recorded for a precedent;
And many an error, by the same example,
Will rush into the state: it can not be.

Shylock—A Daniel come to judgment! Yea, a Daniel!
O wise young judge, how do I honor thee!

Portia—I pray you, let me look upon the bond.

Shylock—Here 'tis, most reverend doctor; here it is.

Portia—Shylock, there's thrice thy money offered thee.

Shylock—An oath, an oath, I have an *oath* in heaven:
Shall I lay perjury upon my soul?
No, not for Venice.

Portia—Why, this bond is forfeit;
And lawfully by this the Jew may claim
A pound of flesh, to be by him cut off
Nearest the merchant's heart. Be *merciful;*
Take *thrice* thy money; bid me *tear* the bond.

Shylock—When it is paid according to the tenor.
It doth appear, you are a *worthy* judge;

You know the *law;* your exposition
Hath been most sound. I charge you by the **law,**
Whereof you are a well deserving pillar,
Proceed to judgment: by my soul I swear,
There is no power in the tongue of man
To alter me. I stay here on my *bond.*
　　Antonio—Most heartily do I beseech the court
To give the judgment.
　　Portia—Why, then, thus it is:
You must prepare your bosom for his knife.
　　Shylock—O noble judge! O excellent young **man!**
　　Portia—For the intent and purpose of the law
Hath full relation to the penalty,
Which here appeareth due upon the bond.
　　Shylock—'T is very true: O wise and upright judge!
How much more elder art thou than thy looks!
　　Portia—Therefore, lay bare your bosom.
　　Shylock—Ay, his breast;
So says the bond—doth it not, noble judge?—
Nearest his heart; those are the very words.
　　Portia—It is so. Are there balance here, to weigh
The flesh?
　　Shylock—I have them ready.
　　Portia—Have by some surgeon, Shylock,—on your
　　charge,—
To stop his wounds, lest he do bleed to death.
　　Shylock—Is it so nominated in the bond?
　　Portia—It is not so expressed; but what of that?
'T were good you do so much for *charity.*
　　Shylock—I can not find it; 't is not in the bond.
　　Portia—Come, merchant, have you anything to say?
　　Antonio—But little; I am armed, and well prepared
Give me your hand, Bassanio! fare you well!
Grieve not that I am fallen to this for you;

For herein fortune shows herself more kind
Than is her custom : it is still her use,
To let the wretched man outlive his wealth ;
To view, with hollow eye and wrinkled brow,
An age of poverty ; from which lingering penance
Of such misery doth she cut me off.
Commend me to your honorable wife :
Tell her the process of Antonio's end ;
Say, how I loved you ; speak me fair in death ;
And, when the tale is told, bid her be judge,
Whether Bassanio had not once a love.
Repent not you that you shall lose your friend ;
And he repents not that he pays your debt ;
For, if the Jew do cut but deep enough,
I 'll pay it instantly with all my heart.

    Portia—A pound of that same merchant's flesh is thine ;
The court awards it, and the law doth give it.

    Shylock—Most rightful judge !

    Portia—And you must cut this flesh from off his breast ;
The law allows it, and the court awards it.

    Shylock—Most learned judge ! A sentence ! come, pre-
        pare.

    Portia—Tarry a little—there is something else—
This bond doth give thee here no jot of blood ;
The words expressly are, a pound of flesh.
Take then thy bond ; take thou thy pound of flesh ;
But, in the cutting it, if thou dost shed
One drop of Christian blood, thy lands and goods
Are, by the laws of Venice, confiscate
Unto the state of Venice.

    Gratiano—O upright judge !—Mark, Jew !—O learned
        judge !

    Shylock—Is that the law ?

    Portia—Thyself shall see the act :
For, as thou urgest justice, be assured
Thou shalt have justice, more than thou desirest.

Gratiano—O learned judge !—Mark, Jew !—a learned
judge !

Shylock—I take this offer, then : pay the bond thrice,
And let the Christian go.

Bassanio—Here is the money.

Portia—Soft ;

The Jew shall have all justice—soft !—no haste—
He shall have nothing but the penalty.

Gratiano—O Jew ! an upright judge ! a learned judge !

Portia—Therefore prepare thee to cut off the flesh.
Shed thou no blood ; nor cut thou less, nor more,
But a just pound of flesh. If thou takest more,
Or less than just a pound—be it but so much
As makes it light or heavy in the substance,
Or the division of the twentieth part
Of one poor scruple—nay, if the scale do turn
But in the estimation of a hair—
Thou diest, and all thy goods are confiscate.

Gratiano—A second Daniel—a Daniel, Jew !
Now, infidel, I have thee on the hip.

Portia—Why doth the Jew pause ? take thy forfeiture

Shylock—Give me my principal and let me go.

Bassanio—I have it ready for thee ; here it is.

Portia—He hath refused it in the open court ;
He shall have merely justice, and his bond.

Gratiano—A Daniel, still say I ! a second Daniel !
I thank thee, Jew, for teaching me that word.

Shylock—Shall I not have barely my principal ?

Portia—Thou shalt have nothing but the forfeiture,
To be so taken at thy peril, Jew.

Shylock—Why, then the devil give him good of it!
I'll stay no longer question.

Portia—Tarry, Jew ;
The law hath yet another hold on you.

It is enacted in the laws of Venice,
If it be proved against an alien,
That, by direct or indirect attempts,
He seek the life of any citizen,
The party, 'gainst the which he doth contrive,
Shall seize one half his goods; the other half
Comes to the privy coffer of the state;
And the offender's life lies in the mercy
Of the duke only, 'gainst all other voice.
In which predicament, I say, thou standest;
For it appears, by manifest proceeding,
That indirectly, and directly too,
Thou hast contrived against the very life
Of the defendant; and thou hast incurred
The danger formerly by me rehearsed.
Down, therefore, and beg mercy of the duke.

    Gratiano—Beg, that thou may'st have leave to hang
        thyself;
And yet, thy wealth being forfeit to the state,
Thou hast not left the value of a cord;
Therefore thou must be hanged at the state's charge.

    Duke—That thou shalt see the difference of our spirit,
I pardon thee thy life before thou ask it.
For half thy wealth, it is Antonio's;
The other half comes to the general state.—SHAKSPEARE.

MARK ANTONY SCENE.

Enter BRUTUS *and* CASSIUS, *and a throng of* Citizens.

CITIZEN—We will be satisfied ; let us be satisfied.
 Brutus—Then follow me, and give me audience,
friends.—
Cassius, go you into the other street,
And part the numbers.—
Those that will hear me speak, let them stay here ;
Those that will follow Cassius, go with him ;
And public reasons shall be rendered
Of Cæsar's death.
 1st Cit.   I will hear Brutus speak.
 2d Cit.—I will hear Cassius ; and compare their reasons,
When severally we hear them rendered.

  [*Exit* CASSIUS, *with some of the* Citizens. BRUTUS
  goes into the rostrum.]

 3d Cit.—The noble Brutus is ascended : Silence !
 Bru.—Be patient till the last.
Romans, countrymen, and lovers ! hear me for my cause ;
and be silent, that you may hear : believe me for mine
honor ; and have respect to mine honor, that you may
believe : censure me in your wisdom ; and awake your
senses, that you may the better judge. If there be any
in this assembly, any dear friend of Cæsar's, to him I
say, that Brutus' love to Cæsar was no less than his. If
then that friend demand, why Brutus rose against Cæsar,
this is my answer,—Not that I loved Cæsar less, but that
I loved Rome more. Had you rather Cæsar were living,
and die all slaves ; than that Cæsar were dead, to live all
free men ? As Cæsar loved me, I weep for him ; as he
was fortunate, I rejoice at it : as he was valiant, I honor

him : but, as he was ambitious, I slew him : There are
tears, for his love; joy, for his fortune; honor, for his
valor; and death, for his ambition. Who is here so base,
that would be a bondman? If any, speak; for him have
I offended. Who is here so rude, that would not be a
Roman? If any, speak ; for him have I offended. Who
is here so vile, that will not love his country? If any,
speak ; for him have I offended. I pause for a reply.

Cit.—None, Brutus, none. [*Several speaking at once.*]

Bru.—Then none have I offended. I have done no
more to Cæsar, than you should do to Brutus. The question of his death is enrolled in the Capitol; his glory not
extenuated, wherein he was worthy ; nor his offences
enforced, for which he suffered death.

Enter ANTONY *and others, with* CÆSAR's *body.*

Here comes his body, mourn'd by Mark Antony; who,
though he had no hand in his death, shall receive the
benefit of his dying, a place in the commonwealth; As
which of you shall not? With this I depart; That, as I
slew my best lover for the good of Rome, I have the
same dagger for myself, when it shall please my country
to need my death.

Cit.—Live! Brutus, live! live!

1st Cit.—Bring him with triumph home unto his house.

2d Cit.—Give him a statue with his ancestors.

3d Cit.—Let him be Cæsar.

4th Cit.   Cæsar's better parts
Shall now be crown'd in Brutus.

1st Cit.—We 'll bring him to his house with shouts
and clamors.

Bru.—My countrymen,—

2d Cit.—Peace; silence ! Brutus speaks.

1st Cit.—Peace. ho !

Bru.—Good countrymen, let me depart alone,
And, for my sake, stay here with Antony:
Do grace to Cæsar's corpse, and grace his speech
Tending to Cæsar's glories ; which Mark Antony,
By our permission, is allow'd to make.
I do entreat you, not a man depart,
Save I alone, till Antony have spoke.   [*Exit.*]
  1*st Cit.*—Stay, ho ! and let us hear Mark Antony.
  3*d Cit.*—Let him go up into the public chair ;
We 'll hear him : Noble Antony, go up.
  Ant.—For Brutus' sake, I am beholden to you.
  4*th Cit.*—What does he say of Brutus ?
  3*d Cit.*   He says, for Brutus' sake,
He finds himself beholden to us all.
  4*th Cit.*—' T were best he speak no harm of Brutus here.
  1*st Cit.*—This Cæsar was a tyrant.
  3*d Cit.*   Nay, that 's certain :
We are bless'd that Rome is rid of him.
  2*d Cit.*—Peace ; let us hear what Antony can say.
  Ant.—You gentle Romans,—
  Cit.   Peace, ho ! let us hear him.
  Ant.—Friends, Romans, countrymen, lend me your ears;
I come to bury Cæsar, not to praise him.
The evil that men do, lives after them ;
The good is oft interred with their bones ;
So let it be with Cæsar.   The noble Brutus
Hath told you, Cæsar was ambitious :
If it were so, it was a grievous fault ;
And grievously hath Cæsar answer'd it.
Here, under leave of Brutus, and the rest,
(For Brutus is an honorable man ;
So are they all, all honorable men ;)
Come I to speak in Cæsar's funeral.
He was my friend, faithful and just to me :

But Brutus says, he was ambitious;
And Brutus is an honorable man.
He hath brought many captives home to Rome,
Whose ransoms did the general coffers fill:
Did this in Cæsar seem ambitious?
When that the poor have cried, Cæsar hath wept:
Ambition should be made of sterner stuff;
Yet Brutus says, he was ambitious;
And Brutus is an honorable man.
You all did see, that on the Lupercal,
I thrice presented him a kingly crown,
Which he did thrice refuse.   Was this ambition?
Yet Brutus says he was ambitious;
And, sure, he is an honorable man.
I speak not to disprove what Brutus spoke,
But here I am to speak what I do know.
You all did love him once; not without cause;
What cause withholds you then to mourn for him?
O judgment, thou art fled to brutish beasts,
And men have lost their reason!—Bear with me;
My heart is in the coffin there with Cæsar,
And I must pause till it come back to me.

   1st Cit.—Methinks, there is much reason in his sayings

   2d Cit.—If thou consider rightly of the matter,
Cæsar has had great wrong.

   3d Cit.   Has he, masters?
I fear, there will a worse come in his place

   4th Cit.—Mark'd ye his words?   He would not take
           the crown;
Therefore, 't is certain he was not ambitious.

   1st Cit.—If it be found so, some will dear abide it.

   2d Cit.—Poor soul! his eyes are red as fire with
           weeping.

   3d Cit.—There's not a nobler man in Rome, than
           Antony.

4th Cit.—Now mark him, he begins again to speak.

Ant.—But yesterday, the word of Cæsar might
Have stood against the world : now lies he there,
And none so poor to do him reverence.
O masters! if I were dispos'd to stir
Your hearts and minds to mutiny and rage,
I should do Brutus wrong, and Cassius wrong,
Who, you all know, are honorable men :
I will not do them wrong ; I rather choose
To wrong the dead, to wrong myself, and you,
Than I will wrong such honorable men.
But here 's a parchment, with the seal of Cæsar,
I found it in his closet, 't is his will :
Let but the commons hear this testament,
(Which, pardon me, I do not mean to read,)
And they would go and kiss dead Cæsar's wounds,
And dip their napkins in his sacred blood ;
Yea, beg a hair of him for memory,
And, dying, mention it within their wills,
Bequeathing it, as a rich legacy,
Unto their issue.

    4th Cit.—We 'll hear the will : Read it, Mark Antony.

    Cit.—The will, the will ; we will hear Cæsar's will.

    Ant.—Have patience, gentle friends, I must not read it;
It is not meet you know how Cæsar loved you.
You are not wood, you are not stones, but men ;
And, being men, hearing the will of Cæsar,
It will inflame you, it will make you mad :
'T is good you know not that you are his heirs;
For if you should, O, what would come of it !

    4th Cit.—Read the will ; we will hear it, Antony;
You shall read us the will ; Cæsar's will.

    Ant.—Will you be patient ? Will you stay a while?
I have o'ershot myself, to tell you of it.

I fear I wrong the honorable men,
Whose daggers have stabb'd Cæsar : I do fear it.

4th Cit.—They were traitors : Honorable men !

Cit.—The will ! the testament !

2d Cit.—They were villains, murderers : The will, read
    the will !

Ant.—You will compel me then to read the will ?
Then make a ring about the corpse of Cæsar,
And let me show you him that made the will.
Shall I descend ?   And will you give me leave ?

Cit.—Come down.

2d Cit.—Descend.   [*He comes down from the pulpit.*]

3d Cit.—You shall have leave.

4th Cit.—A ring ; stand round.

1st Cit.—Stand from the hearse, stand from the body.

2d Cit.—Room for Antony ;—most noble Antony.

Ant.—Nay, press not so upon me ; stand far off.

Cit.—Stand back ! room ! bear back !

Ant.—If you have tears, prepare to shed them now.
You all do know this mantle : I remember
The first time ever Cæsar put it on ;
'T was on a summer's evening, in his tent ;
That day he overcame the Nervii :—
Look ! in this place ran Cassius' dagger through :
See, what a rent the envious Casca made :
Through this, the well-beloved Brutus stabb'd ;
And, as he pluck'd his cursed steel away,
Mark how the blood of Cæsar follow'd it,
As rushing out of doors, to be resolved
If Brutus so unkindly knock'd, or no ;
For Brutus, as you know, was Cæsar's angel :
Judge, O you gods, how dearly Cæsar lov'd him !
This was the most unkindest cut of all :
For when the noble Cæsar saw him stab,

Ingratitude, more strong than traitors' arms,
Quite vanquished him : then burst his mighty heart;
And, in his mantle muffling up his face,
Even at the base of Pompey's statue,
Which all the while ran blood, great Cæsar fell.
O, what a fall was there, my countrymen !
Then I, and you, and all of us fell down,
Whilst bloody treason flourish'd over us.
O, now you weep ; and, I perceive, you feel
The dint of pity : these are gracious drops.
Kind souls, what weep you, when you but behold
Our Cæsar's vesture wounded ?   Look you here,
Here is himself, marr'd, as you see, with traitors.

 1st Cit.—O piteous spectacle !
 2d Cit.—O noble Cæsar !
 3d Cit.—O woful day !
 4th Cit.—O traitors, villains !
 1st Cit.—O most bloody sight !
 2d Cit.—We will be revenged : revenge ; about, —
seek,—burn,—fire,—kill,—slay !—let not a traitor live.
 Ant.—Stay, countrymen.
 1st Cit.—Peace there :—Hear the noble Antony.
 2d Cit.—We 'll hear him, we 'll follow him, we 'll die
  with him.
 Ant.—Good friends, sweet friends, let me not stir you up
To such a sudden flood of mutiny.
They, that have done this deed, are honorable :
What private griefs they have, alas ! I know not,
That made them do 't ; they are wise and honorable,
And will, no doubt, with reasons answer you.
I come not, friends, to steal away your hearts ;
I am no orator, as Brutus is ;
But as you know me all, a plain blunt man,
That love my friend, and that they know full well

That gave me public leave to speak of him.
For I have neither wit, nor words, nor worth,
Action, nor utterance, nor the power of speech,
To stir men's blood: I only speak right on;
I tell you that which you yourselves do know;
Show you sweet Cæsar's wounds, poor, poor dumb mouths,
And bid them speak for me: But were I Brutus
And Brutus Antony, there were an Antony
Would ruffle up your spirits, and put a tongue
In every wound of Cæsar, that should move
The stones of Rome to rise and mutiny.

   Cit.—We'll mutiny.

   1*st Cit.*—We'll burn the house of Brutus.

   3*d Cit.*—Away then, come, seek the conspirators.

   Ant.—Yet hear me, countrymen; yet hear me speak.

   Cit.—Peace, ho! Hear Antony, most noble Antony.

   Ant.—Why, friends, you go to do you know not what:
Wherein hath Cæsar thus deserv'd your loves?
Alas, you know not—I must tell you then:—
You have forgot the will I told you of.

   Cit.—Most true; the will:—let's stay, and hear the will.

   Ant.—Here is the will, and under Cæsar's seal.
To every Roman citizen he gives,
To every several man, seventy-five drachmas.

   2*d Cit.*—Most noble Cæsar!—we'll revenge his **death.**

   3*d Cit.*—O royal Cæsar!

   Ant.—Hear me with patience.   •

   Cit.—Peace, ho!

   Ant.—Moreover, he hath left you all his **walks;**
His private arbors, and new-planted orchards,
On this side Tiber; he hath left them you,
And to your heirs forever; common pleasures,
To walk abroad, and recreate yourselves.
Here was a Cæsar! When comes such another?

1*st Cit.*—Never, never!—Come, away, away!
We'll burn his body in the holy place,
And with the brands fire the traitors' houses.
Take up the body.   [*Exeunt* Citizens *with the body.*]
  Ant.—Now let it work! Mischief, thou art afoot,
Take thou what course thou wilt!—SHAKSPEARE.

THE QUARREL OF BRUTUS AND CASSIUS.

JULIUS CÆSAR.—*Act* IV. *Scene* III.

CASSIUS—That you have wronged me doth appear
    in this :
You have condemned and noted Lucius Pella
For taking bribes here of the Sardians ;
Wherein my letters, praying on his side,
Because I knew the man, were slighted off.
  Brutus—You wronged yourself to write in such a case.
  Cassius—In such a time as this, it is not meet
That every nice offence should bear its comment.
  Brutus—Yet let me tell you, Cassius, you yourself
Are much condemned to have an itching palm,
To sell and mart your offices for gold
To undeservers.
  Cassius—I an itching palm?
You know that you are Brutus that speak this,
Or, by the gods, this speech were else your last.
  Brutus—The name of Cassius honors this corruption,
And chastisement doth therefore hide its head.
  Cassius—Chastisement!
  Brutus—Remember March, the Ides of March re-
    member!

Did not great Julius bleed for justice' sake?
What villain touched his body, that did stab,
And not for justice?   What, shall one of us,
That struck the foremost man in all this world
But for supporting robbers; shall we now
Contaminate our fingers with base bribes,
And sell the mighty space of our large honors,
For so much trash as may be grasped thus?
I had rather be a dog, and bay the moon
Than such a Roman.
  Cassius—Brutus, bay not me.
I'll not endure it: you forget yourself,
To hedge me in; I am a soldier, I,
Older in practice, abler than yourself
To make conditions.
  Brutus—Go to; you are not, Cassius.
  Cassius—I am.
  Brutus—I say you are not.
  Cassius—Urge me no more, I shall forget myself;
Have mind upon your health, tempt me no further.
  Brutus—Away, slight man!
  Cassius—Is 't possible?
  Brutus—Hear me, for I will speak.
Must I give way and room to your rash choler?
Shall I be frighted when a madman stares?
  Cassius—O ye gods! ye gods! must I endure all this?
  Brutus—All this?   Ay, more; fret till your **proud**
   heart break;
Go, show your slaves how choleric you are,
And make your bondmen tremble.   Must I budge?
Must I observe you?   Must I stand and crouch
Under your testy humor?   By the gods,
You shall digest the venom of your spleen,
Though it do split you; for, from this day forth,

I 'll use you for my mirth, yea, for my laughter,
When you are waspish.
 Cassius—Is it come to this?
 Brutus—You say you are a better soldier :
Let it appear so ; make your vaunting true,
And it shall please me well ; for mine own part
I shall be glad to learn of noble men.
 Cassius—You wrong me every way ; you wrong me,
  Brutus ;
I said, an elder soldier, not a better ;
Did I say " better " ?
 Brutus—If you did, I care not.
 Cassius—When Cæsar lived, he durst not so have
  moved me.
 Brutus—Peace, peace ! you durst not so have tempted
  him.
 Cassius—I durst not !
 Brutus—No.
 Cassius—What ?   Durst not tempt him ?
 Brutus—For your life, you durst not.
 Cassius—Do not presume too much upon my love ;
I may do that I shall be sorry for.
 Brutus—You have done that you should be sorry for.
There is no terror, Cassius, in your threats ;
For I am armed so strong in honesty
That they pass by me as the idle wind,
Which I respect not.   I did send to you
For certain sums of gold, which you denied me ;
For I can raise no money by vile means ;
Ye gods !   I had rather coin my heart,
And drop my blood for drachmas, than to wring
From the hard hands of peasants their vile trash
By any indirection.   I did send
To you for gold to pay my legions,

Which you denied me : was that done like Cassius?
Should I have answered Caius Cassius so ?
When Marcus Brutus grows so covetous,
To lock such rascal counters from his friends,
Be ready, gods, with all your thunderbolts ;
Dash him in pieces.

    Cassius—I denied you not.

    Brutus—You did.

    Cassius—I did not : he was but a fool
That brought my answer back.   Brutus hath rived my
       heart.
A friend should bear his friend's infirmities,
But Brutus makes mine greater than they are.

    Brutus—I do not, till you practice them on me.

    Cassius—You love me not.

    Brutus—I do not like your faults.

    Cassius—A friendly eye could never see such faults.

    Brutus—A flatterer's would not, though they do appear
As huge as high Olympus.

    Cassius—Come, Antony, and young Octavius, come,
Revenge yourselves alone on Cassius,
For Cassius is aweary of the world :
Hated by one he loves ; braved by his brother ;
Checked like a bondman ; all his faults observed,
Set in a note-book, learned, and conned by rote,
To cast into my teeth.   Oh, I could weep
My spirit from mine eyes !   There is my dagger,
And here my naked breast ; within, a heart
Dearer than Plutus' mine, richer than gold :
If that thou be 'st a Roman, take it forth ;
I, that denied thee gold, will give my heart :
Strike, as thou didst at Cæsar ; for, I know,
When thou didst hate him worst, thou lovedst him better
Than ever thou lovedst Cassius.

Brutus—Sheathe your dagger :
Be angry when you will, it shall have scope;
Do what you will, dishonor shall be humor.
O Cassius, you are yoked with a lamb
That carries anger as the flint bears fire :
Who, much enforced, shows a hasty spark,
And straight is cold again.
  Cassius—Hath Cassius lived
To be but mirth and laughter to his Brutus,
When grief or blood ill-tempered vexeth him?
  Brutus—When I spoke that, I was ill-tempered, too.
  Cassius—Do you confess so much? Give me your hand
  Brutus—And my heart, too.
  Cassius—O Brutus!
  Brutus—What's the matter?
  Cassius—Have you not love enough to bear with me,
When that rash humor which my mother gave me
Makes me forgetful?
  Brutus—Yes, Cassius ; and, from henceforth,
When you are over-earnest with your Brutus,
He'll think your mother chides, and leave you so.

SHAKSPEARE.

SONGS OF SEVEN.

SEVEN TIMES ONE.—CHILDHOOD.

Arrange as for a tableau—a garden scene, which you may prepare with evergreens and pots of flowers, which may be borrowed or made up for the occasion, a rustic chair, a large garden vase, with trailing vines, and any thing else suitable and available. There must be a background of evergreen trees, or such other greenery as you can command. If it is in the winter, a few artificial flowers can be fastened to the plants.

In selecting a child for this recitation, have regard to talent rather than beauty. Any child will look well enough, but few have the talent to recite this poetry. Take some little girl with a clear, flexible voice, good natural intonation, and genius for reading. In

training her, the first requisite is that she speak every word distinctly, and loud enough to be audible to the listeners; and with
this accuracy of pronunciation there must be nothing stiff or me-
chanical in rendering the sentiment of the poem. If you can make
the child feel that she is that little girl among the flowers, she will
do it all sweetly and naturally. The recitation will be the most effective if she can be taught to recite as if talking to herself, with
some appropriate action. For instance, she enters with a skipping-
rope, or hoop, in her hands, or drawing a doll's wagon. As she
comes down the path to the foot of the stage, she drops her play-
things, looks closely at the leaves—brushes her hand over them to
see if they are wet, then says the first line—

> " There 's no dew left on the daisies and clover; "

then looking up at the sky—

> " There 's no rain left in heaven ; "

then, in a congratulatory way, as if she had finished her work for
that day, and was glad of it—

> " I 've said my ' seven times ' over and over "—

then the last line, with a nod of the head at each word, and the in-
variable sing-song that accompanies the multiplication table—

> " Seven—times—one—are—seven."

In the same manner through all the stanzas. When she says, " Oh,
velvet bee, you 're a dusty fellow," let her peer into some flower,
and then start back, as if she saw the bee in the flower. All such
pretty gestures add much to the effect. But unless the child can do
these gracefully and naturally, they had better not be attempted.

THERE 'S no dew left on the daisies and clover,
  There 's no rain left in heaven.;
I 've said my " seven times " over and over,
  Seven times one are seven.

I am old, so old I can write a letter ;
  My birthday lessons are done ;
The lambs play always, they know no better:
  They are only one times one.

Oh, moon ! in the night I have seen you sailing
  And shining so round and low ;
You were bright! ah bright ! but your light is failing—
  You are nothing now but a bow.

You moon, have you done something wrong in heaven,
That God has hidden your face?
I hope, if you have, you will soon be forgiven,
And shine again in your place.

Oh, velvet bee, you 're a dusty fellow,
You 've powdered your legs with gold!
Oh, brave marsh-mary buds, rich and yellow,
Give me your money to hold!

Oh, columbine, open your folded wrapper,
Where two twin turtle-doves dwell!
Oh, cuckoo-pint, toll me the purple clapper
That hangs in your clear green bell!

And show me your nest, with the young ones in it;
I will not steal them away;
I am old! you may trust me, linnet, linnet—
I am seven times one to-day.

SEVEN TIMES TWO.—ROMANCE.

The same garden scene. A disordered pile of school-books and
slates on the rustic seat. The garden vase should be standing near
the front, and near it, perhaps lounging carelessly upon it, the
school-girl of fourteen. She should be dressed in white, a garden
hat or a long-stemmed flower in her hand. She stands there when
the curtain rises, then lifting her head, looking upward and away,
as if she heard the bells and saw the steeple, she begins to recite.
This poem, as indeed the whole series, is soliloquy, and the per-
fect effect can not be obtained unless it be recited as if unconscious
of the audience. This unconsciousness is one of the finest effects of
genius, and must be, in a certain way, *real*, and not assumed. If the
girl reciting thinks more of herself than of the poetry, it will be impossible to do it well; but if she has genius to appreciate the poem,
to become imbued with its spirit, she will interpret it truly. Very
few gestures are necessary; a looking up toward the steeple when
she speaks to the bells, or a careless swinging of her garden hat, a
toss of her head or a shrug of her shoulders, when it comes in naturally, will be appropriate and pretty.

You bells in the steeple, ring, ring out your changes,
How many soever they be,
And let the brown meadow-lark's note, as he ranges,
Come over, come over to me.

Yet birds' clearest carol, by fall or by swelling,
  No magical sense conveys,
And bells have forgotten their old art of telling
  The fortune of future days.

" Turn again, turn again," once they rung cheerily
  While a boy listened alone;
Made his heart yearn again, musing so wearily
  · All by himself on a stone.

Poor bells! I forgive you; your good days are over.
  And mine, they are yet to be;
No listening, no longing shall aught, aught discover:
  You leave the story to me.

The foxglove shoots out of the green matted heather,
  And hangeth her hoods of snow;
She was idle, and slept till the sunshiny weather;
  Oh, children take long to grow.

I wish, and I wish that the spring would go faster,
  Nor long summer bide so late;
And I could grow on like the foxglove and aster,
  For some things are ill to wait.

I wait for the day when dear hearts shall discover,
  While dear hands are laid on my head;
" The child is a woman, the book may close over,
  For all the lessons are said."

I wait for my story—the birds can not sing it,
  Not one, as he sits on the tree;
The bells can not ring it, but long years, oh, bring it!
  Such as I wish it to be.

SEVEN TIMES THREE.—LOVE.

Same garden scene, with subdued light, as near like moonlight as
possible. A young lady, dressed in white, recites the poem. The
same care must be taken that, while the audience hear every word
distinctly, she does not seem to speak to the audience. Let her remember she is talking to herself, to the night, to the flowers, and to
the absent lover, who is late in coming.

I leaned out of window, I smelt the white clover,
Dark, dark was the garden, I saw not the gate;
" Now, if there be footsteps, he comes, my one lover—
Hush, nightingale, hush! Oh, sweet nightingale, wait
　　　Till I listen and hear
　　　If a step draweth near,
　　　For my love he is late!

" The skies in the darkness stoop nearer and nearer,
A cluster of stars hangs like fruit in the tree,
The fall of the water comes sweeter, comes clearer:
To what art thou listening, and what dost thou see?
　　　Let the star-clusters glow,
　　　Let the sweet waters flow,
　　　And cross quickly to me.

" You night-moths that hover where honey brims over
From sycamore blossoms, or settle, or sleep;
You glow-worms shine out, and the pathway discover
To him that comes darkling along the rough steep.
　　　Ah, my sailor, make haste,
　　　For the time runs to waste,
　　　And my love lieth deep—

" Too deep for swift telling: and yet, my one lover,
I've conned thee an answer, it waits thee to-night."
By the sycamore passed he, and through the white clover,
　　　Then all the sweet speech I had fashioned took flight:

But I'll love him more, more
Than e'er wife loved before,
Be the days dark or bright.

SEVEN TIMES FOUR.—MATERNITY.

The garden scene, brilliantly lighted. Seated upon the garden
bench, the mother in a white dress and matronly cap, weaving a
garland of flowers; one or two little children are seated at her feet:
two others, with flowers in their aprons, stand at her knee. They
hand the flowers to the mother, one by one. As she takes them,
she exclaims to the children:

> "Heigh ho! daisies and buttercups!
> Mother shall thread them a daisy chain;
> Sing them a song of the pretty hedge-sparrow," etc.

The words, "Heigh ho!" occur several times. She speaks them
with archness and vivacity, laughing and smiling, and nodding at
the children, as if talking baby-talk and nonsense to the little ones.
Sometimes, at the "Heigh ho!" she holds up her garland, throws
back her head, as if looking at the effect, then, shaking it at the
children, she laughs out the words, "Heigh ho!" etc. Sometimes
she leans down and gives one of the children a merry little pat, or
a sudden kiss.

> "Oh, bonny brown sons! oh, sweet little daughters,
> Maybe he thinks on you now."

It is impossible to specify particular gestures; the whole tone and
action of the reciter must illustrate what the words so perfectly ex·
press, the sweetness and rich content of happy motherhood.

Heigh ho! daisies and buttercups,
  Fair yellow daffodils, stately and tall,
When the wind wakes how they rock in the grasses,
  And dance with the cuckoo-buds, slender and small:
Here's two bonny boys, and here's mother's own lasses,
  Eager to gather them all.

Heigh ho! daisies and buttercups!
  Mother shall thread them a daisy chain;
Sing them a song of the pretty hedge-sparrow,
  That loved her brown little ones, loved them full fain;
Sing, "Heart thou art wide though the house be but
  narrow—"
    Sing once, and sing it again.

Heigh ho! daisies and buttercups,
Sweet wagging cowslips, they bend and they bow;
A ship sails afar over warm ocean waters,
And haply one musing doth stand at her prow.
Oh, bonny brown sons, oh, sweet little daughters,
Maybe he thinks on you now!

Heigh ho! daisies and buttercups,
Fair yellow daffodils, stately and tall;
A sunshiny world full of laughter and leisure,
And fresh hearts unconscious of sorrow and thrall!
Send down on their pleasure smiles passing its measure,
God that is over us all.

SEVEN TIMES FIVE.—WIDOWHOOD.

In sharp contrast to the preceding merry scene comes the desola-
tion of widowhood. The lights should be somewhat subdued; the
garden scene as before; but to the woman in widow's weeds all
things seem changed. Alone and desolate she leans upon the garden
vase, her accents broken, her gestures slow and painful. As she
speaks the first words, she draws her hand slowly across her ore-
head, as if to wipe out the pain and sad remembrance.
The genius of the reciter must prompt the tones and actior that
best interpret the exquisite pathos of this poem.

I sleep and rest, my heart makes moan
Before I am well awake;
"Let me bleed! oh, let me alone,
Since I must not break!"

For children wake, though fathers sleep,
With a stone at foot and at head:
Oh, sleepless God, forever keep,
Keep both living and dead!

I lift mine eyes, and what to see
But a world happy and fair;
I have not wished it to mourn with me—
Comfort is not there.

Oh, what anear but golden brooms
And a waste of reedy rills;
Oh, what afar but the fine glooms
On the rare blue hills!

I shall not die, but live forlore—
How bitter it is to part!
Oh, to meet thee, my love, once more!—
Oh, my heart, my heart!

No more to hear, no more to see!
Oh, that an echo might wake
And waft one note of thy psalm to me
Ere my heart-strings break!

I should know it, how faint soe'er,
And with angel voices blent;
Oh, once to feel thy spirit anear,
I could be content!

Or once between the gates of gold,
While an angel entering trod,
But once—thee sitting to behold
On the hills of God.

SEVEN TIMES SIX.—GIVING IN MARRIAGE.

The garden scene. A lady richly dressed, as for a daughter's
wedding, enters and recites the poem. As she retires, the curtain
falls; out rises a few moments later upon the tableau of a bridal,
the mother standing in the group. If this tableau is shown twice,
the positions should be changed the second time, the bride and
groom kneeling, instead of standing.

To bear, to nurse, to rear,
To watch, and then to lose:
To see my bright ones disappear,
Drawn up like morning dews—
To bear, to nurse, to rear,
To watch, and then to lose:
This have I done when God drew near
Among his own to choose.

To hear, to heed, to wed,
  And with thy lord depart
In tears that he, as soon as shed,
  Will let no longer smart—
To hear, to heed, to wed,
  This while thou didst I smiled,
For now it was not God who said,
  " Mother, give ME thy child."

Oh, fond, oh, fool, and blind!
  To God I gave with tears,
But when a man like grace would find
  My soul put by her fears—
Oh, fond, oh, fool, and blind!
  God guards in happier spheres,
That man will guard where he did bind
  Is hope for unknown years.

To hear, to heed, to wed,
  Fair lot that maidens choose,
Thy mother's tenderest words are said,
  Thy face no more she views ;
Thy mother's lot, my dear,
  She doth in naught accuse ;
Her lot to bear, to nurse, to rear,
  To love—and then to lose.

SEVEN TIMES SEVEN.—LONGING FOR HOME.

The curtain rises upon the garden scene, the same as at first. A lady, dressed in plain black, with a white cap, enters and comes slowly down the path to the front of the stage. Her form is slightly bowed, her hair is white, her face bears marks of age and suffering; her hands are feeble and old. As she begins the poem, her voice ; s tremulous, but gathers strength as she goes on, until at last it be-comes clear and beautiful, as the vision of her heavenly home lights up her dim sight. As she speaks the last words, the chorus of

"Home, home—sweet, sweet home,
I'm waiting, dear Saviour, for Heaven, my home,"

should be softly sung by a concealed choir. The lady starts with
surprise, stands mute and listening, until the last notes die away
and the curtain falls.

A song of a boat:
There was once a boat on a billow,
Lightly she rocked to her port remote,
And the foam was white in her wake like snow,
And her frail mast bowed when the breeze would blow,
And bent like a wand of willow.

I shaded mine eyes one day when a boat
Went courtesying over the billow;
I marked her course till, a dancing mote,
She faded out on the moonlit foam,
And I stayed behind in the dear loved home;
And my thoughts all day were about the boat
And my dreams upon the pillow.

I pray you hear my song of a boat,
For it is but short;
My boat, you shall find none fairer afloat,
In river or port.

Long I looked out for the lad she bore,
On the open desolate sea,
And I think he sailed to the heavenly shore,
For he came not back to me—
Ah me!

A song of a nest:
There was once a nest in a hollow,
Down in the mosses and knot-grass pressed
Soft and warm, and full to the brim;
Vetches leaned over it, purple and dim,
With buttercup buds to follow.

I pray you hear my song of a nest,
    For it is not long:
You shall never light in a summer quest
    The bushes among—
      Shall never light on a prouder sitter,
      A fairer nestful, nor ever know
      A softer sound than their tender twitter,
      That wind-like did come and go.

I had a nestful once of my own,
    Ah, happy, happy I!
Right dearly I loved them: but when they were grown
    They spread out their wings to fly—
Oh, one after one they flew away
    Far up to the heavenly blue,
To the better country, the upper day,
    And—I wish I was going, too.

I pray you, what is the nest to me,
    My empty nest?
And what is the shore where I stood to see
    My boat sail down to the west?
Can I call that home where I anchor yet,
    Though my good man has sailed?
Can I call that home where my nest was set,
    Now all its hope hath failed?
Nay, but the port where my sailor went,
    And the land where my nestlings be:
There is the home where my thoughts are sent,
    The only home for me!
        Ah me!
      ADAPTED FROM JEAN INGELOW.

ROMEO AND JULIET.

BALCONY SCENE.

R OMEO—He jests at scars that never felt a wound.

JULIET *appears on the Balcony, and sits down.*

But soft! What light through yonder window breaks!
It is the east, and Juliet is the sun!
Arise, fair sun, and kill the envious moon,
Who is already sick and pale with grief,
That thou, her maid, art far more fair than she.
"It is my lady; Oh! it is my love:
Oh, that she knew she were!"
She speaks, yet she says nothing: what of that?
Her eye discourses: I will answer it.
I am too bold. Oh, were those eyes in heaven,
They would through the airy region stream so bright,
That birds would sing, and think it were the morn.
See, how she leans her cheek upon her hand!
Oh, that I were a glove upon that hand,
That I might touch that cheek!

   Juliet—Ah, me!

   Romeo—She speaks, she speaks!
Oh, speak again, bright angel! for thou art
As glorious to this sight, being o'er my head,
As is a winged messenger of heaven
To the up-turned wond'ring eyes of mortals.
When he bestrides the lazy-pacing clouds,
And sails upon the bosom of the air.

   Juliet—Oh, Romeo, Romeo! wherefore art thou Romeo!
Deny thy father, and refuse thy name:
Or, if thou wilt not, be but sworn my love,
And I'll no longer be a Capulet.

   Romeo—Shall I hear more, or shall I speak at this?

Juliet—'Tis but thy name that is my enemy!
What's in a name? That which we call a rose,
By any other name would smell as sweet;
So Romeo would, were he not Romeo called,
Retain that dear perfection which he owes
Without that title! Romeo, quit thy name;
And for that name, which is no part of thee,
Take all myself.

 Romeo—I take thee at thy word!
Call me but love, 1 will forswear my name
And never more be Romeo.

 Juliet—What man art thou, that, thus bescreened in
  night
So stumblest on my counsel?

 Romeo—I know not how to tell thee who I am!
My name, dear saint, is hateful to myself,
Because it is an enemy to thee.

 Juliet—My ears have not yet drunk a hundred words
Of that tongue's uttering, yet I know the sound!
Art thou not Romeo, and a Montague?

 Romeo—Neither, fair saint, if either thee displease.

 Juliet—How cam'st thou hither?—tell me—and for
  what?
The orchard walls are high, and hard to climb;
And the place, death, considering who thou art,
If any of my kinsmen find thee here.

 Romeo—With love's light wings did I o'er-perch these
  walls;
For stony limits cannot hold love out;
And what love can do, that dares love attempt;
Therefore thy kinsmen are no stop to me.

 Juliet—If they do see thee here, they'll murder thee.

 Romeo—Alack, there lies more peril in thine eye,
Than twenty of their swords! look thou but sweet,
And I am proof against their enmity.

Juliet—I would not, for the world, they saw thee here ?
By whose direction found'st thou out this place?

Romeo—By love, who first did prompt me to inquire;
He lent me counsel, and I lent him eyes.
I am no pilot; yet, wert thou as far
As that vast shore washed with the furthest sea,
I would adventure for such merchandise.

Juliet—Thou know'st, the mask of night is on my
　　　face,
Else would a maiden blush bepaint my cheek,
For that which thou hast heard me speak to-night!
Fain would I dwell on form; fain, fain deny
What I have spoke! But farewell compliment!
Dost thou love me? I know thou wilt say—Ay,
And I will take thy word! yet, if thou swear'st,
Thou may'st prove false; at lovers' perjuries
They say, Jove laughs. Oh, gentle Romeo,
If thou dost love, pronounce it faithfully!
Or, if thou think'st I am too quickly won,
I'll frown, and be perverse, and say thee nay,
So thou wilt woo! but else, not for the world.
In truth, fair Montague, I am too fond:
And therefore thou may'st think my 'haviour light!
But trust me, gentleman, I'll prove more true
Than those that have more cunning to be strange.
I should have been more strange, I must confess,
But that thou overheard'st, ere I was 'ware,
My true love's passion; therefore, pardon me,
And not impute this yielding to light love,
Which the dark night has so discovered.

Romeo—Lady, by yonder blessed moon I vow—

Juliet—Oh! swear not by the moon, the inconstant
　　　moon
That monthly changes in her circled orb;

Lest that thy love prove likewise variable.

Romeo—What shall I swear by?

Juliet—Do not swear at all;
Or, if thou wilt, swear by thy gracious self,
Which is the god of my idolatry,
And I'll believe thee.

Romeo—If my true heart's love—

Juliet—Well, do not swear! Although I joy in thee,
I have no joy of this contract to-night;
It is too rash, too unadvised, too sudden,
Too like the lightning, which doth cease to be,
'Ere one can say—It lightens. Sweet, good-night!
This bud of love, by summer's ripening breath,
May prove a beauteous flower when next we meet.
Good-night, good-night!—as sweet repose and rest
Come to thy heart, as that within my breast!

Romeo—Oh, wilt thou leave me so unsatisfied?

Juliet—What satisfaction canst thou have to-night?

Romeo—The exchange of thy love's faithful vow for
mine.

Juliet—I gave thee mine, before thou didst request it;
And yet I would it were to give again.

Romeo—Would'st thou withdraw it? for what purpose,
love?

Juliet—But to be frank, and give it thee again.
My bounty is as boundless as the sea,
My love as deep; the more I give to thee,
The more I have; for both are infinite.
I hear some noise within. Dear love, adieu!

Nurse—[*Within*]—Madam!

Juliet—Anon, good Nurse! Sweet Montague, be true
Stay but a little, I will come again. [*Exit from balcony.*

Romeo—Oh! blessed, blessed night! I am afeard,
Being in night, all this is but a dream,
Too flattering sweet to be substantial.

Re-enter JULIET, *above.*

Juliet—Three words, dear Romeo, and good-night,
      indeed.
If that thy bent of love be honorable,
Thy purpose marriage, send me word to-morrow,
By one that I'll procure to come to thee,
Where, and what time, thou wilt perform the rite;
And all my fortunes at thy foot I'll lay;
And follow thee, my lord, throughout the world.
      Nurse—[*Within*]—Madam!
      Juliet—I come anon!   But, if thou mean'st not well,
I do beseech thee—
      Nurse—[*Within*]—Madam!
      Juliet—By and by, I come!
To cease thy suit, and leave me to my grief.
To-morrow will I send.
      Romeo—So thrive my soul—
      Juliet—A thousand times good-night!
      Romeo—A thousand times the worse, to want thy
      light.   [*Exit.*]

Re-enter JULIET.

Juliet—Hist! Romeo, hist! Oh, for a falconer's voice,
To lure this tassel gentle back again!
Bondage is hoarse, and may not speak aloud;
Else would he fear the cave where Echo lies,
And make her airy tongue more hoarse than mine,
With repetition of my Romeo's name.

ROMEO *entering.*

Romeo—It is my love that calls upon my name!
How silver-sweet sound lovers' tongues by night,
Like softest music to attending ears!
      Juliet—Romeo!
      Romeo—My sweet!

Juliet—At what o'clock to-morrow
Shall I send to thee?
Romeo—At the hour of nine.
Juliet—I will not fail : 'tis twenty years till then.
I have forgot why I did call thee back.
Romeo—Let me stand here till thou remember it.
Juliet—I shall forget, to have thee still stand there,
Rememb'ring how I love thy company.
Romeo—And I'll still stay, to have thee still forget,
Forgetting any other home but this.
Juliet—'Tis almost morning ; I would have thee gone,
And yet no further than a wanton's bird;
Who lets it hop a little from her hand,
And with a silk thread plucks it back again,
So loving-jealous of its liberty.
Romeo—I would I were thy bird.
Juliet—Sweet, so would I!
Yet I should kill thee with much cherishing.
Good-night, good-night! Parting is such sweet sorrow
That I shall say—Good-night, till it be morrow.
                              [*Exit from balcony.*]
Romeo—Sleep dwell upon thine eyes, peace in thy
       breast!
Would I were sleep and peace, so sweet to rest!
Hence will I to my ghostly father's cell;
His help to crave, and my dear hap to tell.
                              SHAKSPEARE.

Shoemaker's Best Selections, No. 1

Compiled by J. W. SHOEMAKER, A. M.

**Late President, and founder of The National School of Elocution and Oratory
200 pages. Cloth binding, 50 cents ; Paper, 30 cents**

In addition to its value as a book of recitations this is an exceedingly good number for school use owing to the great variety of pieces suitable for reading classes. The following pieces are among some of the most valuable ones.

Abraham Lincoln, extract from a eulogy on the martyred president, by Henry Ward Beecher.

Annie and Willie's Prayer, an excellent Christmas piece.

Betsy and I are Out, by Will Carleton.

The Blue and the Gray, for Decoration Day. The ever popular class poem.

The Boys, by Oliver Wendell Holmes.

The Bridge, by Longfellow.

The Charcoal Man, affording excellent opportunities for vocal gymnastics.

The Child Wife, humorous, from David Copperfield.

The Creeds of the Bells, containing splendid opportunities for vocal display.

Crossing the Carry, humorous, by the popular author, "Adirondack" Murray.

Death of Little Joe, and

Death of Little Nell, both pathetic and both from Charles Dickens.

Der Coming Man, German Dialect, by Chas. Follen Adams.

The Dying Christian, excellent for Sunday-school entertainments, by Alexander Pope.

Evening at the Farm, a beautiful pastoral poem, by J. T. Trowbridge.

Experience with European Guides, humorous, by Mark Twain.

Independence Bell, for Fourth of July occasions.

The Irish School Master, a capital Irish Dialect piece.

John Maynard, thrilling and heroic.

Launch of the Ship, by Henry W. Longfellow, excellent for vocal training.

Memory of Washington, for Washington's Birthday, by Edward Everett.

The Modern Cain, a strong temperance recitation.

Nobody's Child, exceedingly pathetic.

The Old Yankee Farmer, Yankee Dialect.

Palmerston and Lincoln, a strong piece of historical literature, by George Bancroft.

Patrick Dolin's Love Letter, Irish Courting.

Pat's Excelsior, Irish parody on the original poem.

A Piece of Bunting,

The Relief of Lucknow, and **The Revolutionary Rising,** strong patriotic selections.

Scrooge and Marley, a most interesting extract from Dickens' Christmas Carol.

The Smack in School, very amusing.

Spartacus to the Gladiators, popular with every school boy.

Uncle Pete's Counsel to the Newly Married, Darkey Dialect.

Why He Wouldn't Sell the Farm, pathetic and patriotic.

William Tell, thrilling and patriotic.

Will the New Year Come To-night, Mamma? pathetic.

THE FOLLOWING GEMS FROM TENNYSON:

Break, Break, Break.

Bugle Song.

The dramatic Charge of the Light Brigade.

Lullaby.

The Old Year and the New, for New Year's. And

THE FOLLOWING SHAKESPEAREAN EXTRACTS:

Hamlet's Instructions to the Players.

The Ghost Scene.

Othello's Apology.

Shoemaker's Best Selections No. 2

Compiled by J. W. SHOEMAKER, A. M.
Late President, and founder of The National School of Elocution and Oratory
200 pages. Cloth binding, 50 cents: Paper, 30 cents

This too, is a good number for use in reading classes. Among the many excellent pieces may be mentioned the following:

Abigail Becker, a thrilling description of a rescue at sea.

Andrew Jackson, a eulogy, and excellent for reading classes, by George Lippard.

Arnold Winkelreid, a dramatic incident in the history of Switzerland.

The Barn Window, good for reading classes, by Lucy Larcom.

The Bells of Shandon, excellent for vocal culture.

The Blacksmith's Story, a thrilling incident as a result of the War of the Rebellion.

Black Ranald, a dramatic recitation by Phœbe Cary.

Buck Fanshaw's Funeral, exceedingly humorous, by Mark Twain.

A Christmas Carol, a pleasing little Christmas poem.

Darius Green and His Flying Machine, humorous, by J. T. Trowbridge.

Dowe's Flat, 1856, a story of the early days of California, by F. Bret Harte.

A Dutchman's Speech at an Institute, German Dialect.

Eva's Death, pathetic, from Uncle Tom's Cabin, by Harriet Beecher Stowe.

Excelsior, a world-wide popular poem, by Henry W. Longfellow.

The Ghosts, extract from Hiawatha, by H. W. Longfellow.

Hezekiah Bedott, an extract from the famous Bedott Papers.

How Mr. Coville Counted the Shingles on His House, by the Danbury News Man. Humorous.

Kentucky Philosophy, sometimes known as the "Watermillion Story," Darky Dialect and very popular.

Liberty and Union, the celebrated speech of Daniel Webster.

Lochinvar's Ride, always popular, by Sir Walter Scott.

Mark Twain and the Interviewer, humorous.

The May Queen, Conclusion, pathetic, by Alfred Tennyson.

Miss Maloney on the Chinese Question, Irish humor, by Mary Mapes Dodge.

The Minute Men of '75, a beautiful patriotic address, by George William Curtis.

Mr. Coville on Danbury, humorous, by the Danbury News Man.

The Nature of True Eloquence, excellent for declamation, by Daniel Webster.

The New Church Organ, spinster characterization, by Will Carleton.

A New Year's Address, a strong prose selection for New Year's occasions, by Dr. Edward Brooks, A. M.

North American Indians, excellent for declamation.

The Old Man in the Model Church, pathetic and excellent for old man characterization.

The Old Clock on the Stairs, containing fine opportunities for voice culture, by Henry W. Longfellow.

Oratory and the Press, good for declamation, by Daniel Dougherty.

Over the Hill to the Poorhouse, pathetic, good opportunities for old woman characterization, by Will Carleton.

The Polish Boy, exceedingly dramatic.

The Puzzled Dutchman, German Dialect.

The Red Jacket, dramatic description of a fire scene.

Rum's Maniac, dramatic; excellent temperance selection.

Schnieder Sees Leah, a German's version of a scene from Leah the Forsaken, very popular.

Sixty-Four and Sixty-Five, a good piece for G. A. R. entertainments.

Socrates Snooks, the humorous experience of a henpecked husband.

The Soldier's Reprieve, a beautiful story in connection with the administration of President Lincoln.

The Spanish Armada, an historic poem of great dramatic opportunities, by T. B. Macaulay.

Washington as a Civilian, for Washington's Birthday.

The Yarn of the Nancy Bell, humorous, a sailor's story, and

THE FOLLOWING SHAKESPEARIAN EXTRACTS:

Cassius Against Cæsar.
Hamlet's Soliloquy.
Wolsey's Fall.

Shoemaker's Best Selections, No. 3

Compiled by J. W. SHOEMAKER, A. M.

Late President, and founder of The National School of Elocution and Oratory

200 pages. Cloth binding, 50 cents; Paper, 30 cents

Many good teaching pieces will be found in this number, also. The following are some of the most popular selections:

Adoon the Lane, a delicious bit of Scotch Dialect.

The American Flag, a fine patriotic piece, by Joseph Rodman Drake.

The Baby's First Tooth, humorous, by the Danbury News Man.

Bardell and Pickwick, the famous trial scene, by Charles Dickens.

The Baron's Last Banquet, dramatic.

The Battle of Beal an' Duine, a strong war poem of Scotland, by Sir Walter Scott.

The Burning Ship, a dramatic description of a ship on fire.

Claudius and Cynthia, a popular dramatic selection, scene in Rome.

The Closing Year, for New Year's, by George D. Prentice.

The Dutchman's Serenade, German Dialect.

The Eagle's Rock, very dramatic.

The Famine, from Hiawatha, by Henry W. Longfellow.

A Florentine Letter, highly dramatic, by Susan Coolidge.

From Exile, dramatic.

The Gladiator, very dramatic, scene in Rome.

Good-night, Papa, a beautiful temperance recitation.

The Haunted House, a dramatic description, by Hood.

The Hypochondriac, humorous.

If I Should Die To-night, spiritual, and suited for Sunday-schools.

The Indian Chief to the White Settler, a popular declamation, by Edward Everett.

Jack and Jill, light humor.

Kit Carson's Ride, a stirring incident of life on the prairie, by Joaquin Miller.

The Kitchen Clock, exceedingly popular, by John Vance Cheney.

Laughin' in Meeting, humorous, by Harriet Beecher Stowe.

Licensed to Sell; or, Little Blossom, temperance.

Lides to Bary Jade, humorous description of a man with a cold in his head.

Little Golden Hair, child characterization.

Maud Muller, always popular, by John G. Whittier.

The Monster Cannon, a dramatic description, by Victor Hugo.

National Monument to Washington, for Washington's Birthday.

Ode on the Passions, a superior teaching piece, especially for voice culture, by Collins.

The Painter of Seville, strong and popular.

Parrhassius and the Captive, very dramatic, by N. P. Willis.

Passing Away, familiar, but good.

Poor Little Jim, a pathetic story of the mines.

The Power of Habit, a striking temperance selection, by John B. Gough.

The Promise, spiritual, good for Sunday-schools.

Reaching the Early Train, humorous, by Max Adler.

Reply to Mr. Corry, forensic oratory, good for teaching, by H. Grattan.

Rock of Ages, very pretty, contains singing parts.

The Senator's Dilemma, humorous, by James De Mille.

The Seven Ages of Man, from Shakespeare.

Signs and Omens, German Dialect.

Tell on His Native Hills, patriotic, a good teaching piece.

The Three Fishers, tender and pathetic, by Charles Kingsley.

Tom Sawyer's Love Affair, humorous, by Mark Twain.

The Two Glasses, temperance, by Ella Wheeler Wilcox.

The Vagabonds, pathetic, dramatic, and a good temperance piece, always acceptable, by J. T. Trowbridge.

Woman, a pleasing tribute to her sex, by Tennyson.

Shoemaker's Best Selections No. 4

Compiled by J. W. SHOEMAKER, A. M.

Late President, and founder of The National School of Elocution and Oratory

200 pages. Cloth binding, 50 cents ; Paper, 30 cents

This issue is characterized by the great number of patriotic pieces which it contains. In addition to this feature the following selections may also be mentioned:

A Man's a Man for a' That, a popular Scotch Dialect poem, by Robert Burns.

The Angels of Buena Vista, a very dramatic battle scene, by John G. Whittier.

The Annuity, humorous, Scotch Dialect.

Aunt Kindly, a good teaching piece on the conversational order, by Theo. Parker.

Ye Baggage Smasher, humorous.

The Battle of Bunker Hill, strong patriotic poem.

Battle Hymn of the Republic, stirring patriotic poem, by Julia Ward Howe.

The Black Horse and His Rider, a fine prose patriotic declamation, by Charles Sheppard.

The Burning Prairie, a dramatic recitation, by Alice Carey.

The Cause of Temperance, a strong temperance piece, by John B. Gough.

Centennial Oration, a fine declamation, and also excellent for teaching purposes, by Henry Armitt Brown.

The Christmas Sheaf, a Norwegian Christmas story.

Columbia, patriotic.

Curfew Must Not Ring To-Night, familiar, but a very popular recitation, by Rose Hartwick Thorpe.

Deacon Munroe's Story, humorous characterization.

The Declaration of Independence, very convenient for Fourth of July occasions, as well as for reference purposes.

Dora, a dramatic descriptive characterization, by Tennyson.

Dot Lambs Wot Mary Haf Got, a parody on the original poem in German Dialect.

The Fire, a dramatic description.

The Gambler's Wife, pathetic and dramatic.

The Ghost, sometimes known as "Abel Law's Ghost," quaint Yankee humor.

Grandmother's Story, an old woman's story of the Battle of Bunker Hill.

The Great Beef Contract, exceedingly humorous, by Mark Twain.

How a Married Man Sews on a Button, humorous, by The Danbury News Man.

Judge Pitman on Various Kinds of Weather, humorous, by Max Adler.

Kentucky Belle, a popular poem, describing an incident of the Civil War, by Constance Fenimore Woolson.

Leap Year Wooing, humorous, by David Macrae.

A Negro Prayer, Darkey Dialect.

No God, a strong moral selection.

Ode to the Deity, a fine oratorical selection, excellent for voice culture.

Ode to the Legislature, a satirical poem, by John G Saxe.

Battle of Lookout Mountain, a thrilling description by George H. Boker.

The Rationalistic Chicken, humorous.

The Raven, old but still given by some of the best readers.

Rienzi's Address, stirring declamation.

Tommy Taft, good for temperance occasions.

Tribute to Washington, for Washington's Birthday.

The Union, a patriotic poem.

Clarence's Dream and Mark Antony Scene. Shakespearean Extracts.

Shoemaker's Best Selections No. 5

Compiled by J. W. SHOEMAKER, A. M.

Late President, and founder of The National School of Elocution and Oratory
200 pages. Cloth binding, 50 cents; Paper, 30 cents

Among the most popular recitations in this number are the following:

The Ager, a humorous description of a sufferer with chills and fever.

Archie Dean, a selection of the coquettish order, by Gail Hamilton.

Bannock-Burn, a stirring bit of Scotch poetry, by Robert Burns.

The Bride of the Greek Isle, a dramatic recitation, by Mrs. Hemans.

The Brook, a popular poem, by Tennyson.

Budge's Version of the Flood, child characterization, very amusing, by John Habberton.

Catiline's Defiance, familiar but always a popular declamation.

Course of Love Too Smooth, the amusing experience of a pair of lovers on a slippery night.

Dedication of Gettysburg Cemetery, the celebrated speech of Abraham Lincoln.

Elder Mr. Weller's Sentiments on Literary Composition, from Pickwick Papers, by Charles Dickens.

Fashionable Singing, a humorous representation of fashionable singers.

The Flood of Years, a strong oratorical selection, excellent for teaching, by William Cullen Bryant.

Good Reading, an extract from an excellent address on the subject of public reading, by John S. Hart.

Hans and Fritz, German Dialect.

He Giveth His Beloved Sleep, a beautiful spiritual poem, by Mrs. Browning.

Heroes of the Land of Penn, patriotic, having especial reference to the early settlers of Pennsylvania, by George Lippard.

How We Hunted a Mouse, humorous.

John and Tibbie's Dispute, Scotch humor.

The Last Hymn, describing a wreck at sea, pathetic and dramatic, part to be sung.

The Leak in the Dyke, a dramatic recitation by Phœbe Cary.

Lost and Found, a pathetic story of the Welsh Mines.

Magdalena; or, the Spanish Duel, humorous and popular, the incident is laid in Spain.

The Maiden Martyr, very pathetic.

Membraneous Croup and the McWilliamses, humorous, by Mark Twain.

Moral Effect of Intemperance, a strong temperance piece, by Henry Ward Beecher.

My Trundle-Bed, pathetic recollections of a mother's teachings.

Old Ironsides, a patriotic tribute to the old frigate, "Constitution," by O. W. Holmes.

Over the Hills and Far Away, a beautiful bit of pathos, by Miss Mulock.

The Prisoner of Chillon, a very dramatic selection, by Byron.

The Puritans, a strong prose description of our forefathers, by T. B Macaulay.

Samantha Smith Becomes Josiah Allen's Wife, humorous, by Josiah Allen's Wife.

The Schoolmaster's Guests, a humorous characterization, by Will Carleton.

The Swell's Soliloquy, impersonation of a dude.

Swallowing a Fly, a bit of prose, characteristic of the author, T. De Witt Talmage.

Tramp, Tramp, Tramp, a stirring temperance piece, by J. G. Holland.

Uncle Daniel's Introduction to a Mississippi Steamer, one of the best negro dialect pieces ever written, by Clemens and Warner.

Why Biddie and Pat Married, an amusing Irish dialect recitation.

Man's Ingratitude. and

Prince Henry and Falstaff, Shakespearean extracts.

Shoemaker's Best Selections, No. 6

Compiled by J. W. SHOEMAKER, A. M.

Late President, and founder of The National School of Elocution and Oratory

200 pages. Cloth binding, 50 cents ; Paper, 30 cents

The following may be mentioned as among some of the most effec‑ tive recitations:

Artemus Ward's London Lecture, one of the best humorous pieces ever written.

Asleep at the Switch, a thrilling inci‑ dent in the experience of a switch tender.

The Battle of Ivry, a standard dra‑ matic recitation, by T. B. Macaulay.

The Bridge of Sighs, a popular pathetic poem, by Thomas Hood.

Brother Anderson's Sermon, a superior negro dialect recitation, by Thomas K. Beecher.

The Children's Hour, a poetic descrip‑ tion of the author's children, Henry W. Longfellow.

A Day at Niagara, a humorous descrip‑ tion of a visit to Niagara Falls, by Mark Twain.

The Deserted House, a beautiful de‑ scription of life and death, by Tenny‑ son.

Doctor Marigold, sometimes known as the cheap Jack, excellent opportuni‑ ties for characterization, by Charles Dickens.

The Dukite Snake, an Australian bush‑ man's story, extremely dramatic, by J. Boyle O'Reilly.

Easter Morning, a pleasing Easter poem.

Eve and the Serpent, a Frenchman's idea of the fall of man, humorous.

Extract from the Last Days of Hercu‑ laneum, a fine dramatic description.

Father Phil's Collection, this is one of the best Irish dialect recitations, and is given by some of the most promi‑ nent readers.

Getting Under Way, an amusing de‑ scription of sea-sickness, by Mark Twain.

The Green Mountain Justice, humor‑ ous.

Jane Conquest, the incident is that of a wreck at sea, very dramatic.

The Little Hatchet Story, one of the most popular humorous recitations in print. It is a description of the inci‑ dent of George Washington and the cherry tree.

Miss Edith Helps T h i n g s A l o n g, a humorous characterization of a pert child, by Bret Harte.

Nae Luck Aboot the House, a pleasing Scotch poem.

The Old Sergeant, a pathetic story of the Civil War.

The Palmetto and the Pine, a figura‑ tive description of the North and South.

Relentless Time, excellent for teaching by Henry W. Longfellow.

The Ride of Jennie McNeal, a story of colonial days, by Will Carleton.

Robert of Lincoln, introducing bird songs, by William Cullen Bryant.

Satan and the Grog Seller, a fine tem perance piece.

School Called, a pleasing poem illus trative of school life.

Song in the Night, an amusing sleep‑ ing-car incident introducing snoring

St. John, the Aged, a beautiful spirit ual poem.

Thanatopsis, always popular, excel‑ lent for teaching, by William Cullen Bryant.

A Thanksgiving, a pleasing poem for Thanksgiving, by Lucy Larcom.

Tom, a story of how a dog saves the life of a child in a fire, by Constance Fenimore Woolson.

Valley Forge, a fine oratorical selection good for teaching, by Henry Armitt Brown.

Zekle, Yankee courting, by James Rus sell Lowell.

The Dagger Scene, and

From the Tragedy of King John Shakespearean Extracts.

Shoemaker's Best Selections No. 7

Compiled by J. W. SHOEMAKER, A. M.

Late President, and founder of The National School of Elocution and Oratory
200 pages. Cloth binding, 50 cents ; Paper, 30 cents

While it is the aim to make one number as good as another, this issue has always been one of the most popular of the series. Following are some of the most attractive selections :

The Death of the Old Year, appropriate for New Year's, by Tennyson.

The American War, a fine forensic selection, by Lord Chatham.

A Royal Princess, a strong dramatic recitation, by Christina Rossetti.

Sister and I, pathetic and extremely popular.

The Death of Nelson, a good teaching piece, by Robert Southey.

The Night Before Christmas, always popular for Christmas entertainments.

The Night After Christmas, a humorous sequel to the foregoing selection.

A Parody, being a parody on Cassabianca ; or, The Boy Stood on the Burning Deck.

The Crescent and the Cross, a beautiful contrast between Christianity and Mohammedism, by T. B. Aldrich.

Reflections on Westminster Abbey, excellent literature, good for teaching, by Washington Irving.

Our Traveled Parson, humorous, by Will Carleton.

Daisy's Faith, popular child characterization.

How Tom Sawyer Whitewashed His Fence, humorous, by Mark Twain.

Cuddle Doon, a pleasing bit of Scotch Dialect.

The Death of the Owd 'Squire, a fine dramatic piece. Scene in Yorkshire.

Mine Katrine, German Dialect, by Charles Follen Adams.

The Voice in the Twilight, good for Sunday-schools, by Mrs. Herrick Johnson.

The Ship of Faith, an exceedingly good Negro Dialect piece.

Mount Blanc Before Sunrise, a beautiful oratorical poem, good for teaching, by S. T. Coleridge.

Surly Tim's Trouble, a pathetic and very popular piece; used by the best readers ; Lancashire Dialect.

The Village Blacksmith, always popular, by Henry W. Longfellow.

Tom's Little Star, a humorous poem describing the experience of a stagestruck woman.

Marco Bozzaris, old but good, an excellent teaching piece, by Fitz-Greene Halleck.

Fair Play for Women, an appeal for the rights of woman, by George William Curtis.

Masters of the Situation, a superior teaching selection, by James T. Fields

Lighthouse May, an excellent selection, showing the heroism of a lighthouse keeper.

A Model Discourse, humorous, sometimes known as the Old Mother Hubbard Sermon.

The South Wind, a pleasing description, good teaching piece, by Henry W. Longfellow.

The Wounded Soldier, pathetic ; the incident is that of a dying soldier. Very popular.

The Owl-Critic, very clever humor, by James T. Fields.

The Leper, a strong dramatic recitation by N. P. Willis.

That Hired Girl, humorous.

Old Robin, how a horse saves his master from moral ruin, by J. T. Trowbridge.

Hannah Binding Shoes, a beautiful and pathetic poem, by Lucy Larcom

The Gray Honors the Blue, good for Decoration Day, by Henry H. Watterson.

Paradise, an excellent encore piece.

Widow Brown's Christmas, a pleasing Christmas story.

Shoemaker's Best Selections, No. 8

Compiled by Mrs. J. W. SHOEMAKER

Vice-President of The National School of Elocution and Oratory

200 pages. Cloth binding, 50 cents; Paper, 30 cents

From the many good pieces in this number the following may be mentioned:

After Death, a beautiful spiritual poem, by Edwin Arnold.

Reckoning With the Old Year, for New Year's.

The Defense of Lucknow, a patriotic recitation, by Tennyson.

Nations and Humanity, oratorical, by George William Curtis.

The Emigrant's Story, the main incident is that of a storm on the prairie, very popular, by J. T. Trowbridge.

Mrs. McWilliams and the Lightning, humorous, by Mark Twain.

A Christmas Carol, a magnificent poem; parts to be chanted, by Father Ryan.

The Song of Steam, good for teaching.

Setting a Hen, German Dialect, sometimes known as Sockery Setting a Hen

The Everlasting Memorial, good for Sunday-school entertainments, by Horatius Bonar.

Scene from Leah, the Forsaken, generally known as the Curse Scene.

Grandma Al'as Does, child characterization.

Nebuchadnezzer, Negro Dialect.

The Temperance Question, an excellent temperance piece, by Wendell Phillips

Better in the Morning, very pathetic.

Philosophy of Laughter, a laughing piece

Say Billy, an incident of the Civil War, good for Decoration Day.

The King's Missive, 1661, a story of colonial times, by John G. Whittier.

Blue Sky Somewhere, pathetic.

Coney Island Down der Pay, German Dialect, by Henry Firth Wood.

The Sioux Chief's Daughter, very dra-

matic and exceedingly popular, by Joaquin Miller.

The Bald-Headed Man, very funny, introducing an inquisitive child.

An International Episode, an encore.

The Arrow and the Song, also a pleasing encore piece, by Henry W. Longfellow.

Rest, good for Sunday-schools, by George MacDonald.

Carl, dramatic.

Enoch Arden, an extract from the popular poem of that name, by Tennyson.

The Character of Washington, for Washington's Birthday.

A Practical Young Woman, humorous

Over the Hill from the Poorhouse, a sequel to Over the Hill to the Poorhouse, by Will Carleton.

Peace in God, for Sunday-schools, by Mrs. Harriet Beecher Stowe.

Beecher on Eggs, humorous.

A Tale of the Yorkshire Coast, a pathetic selection in Yorkshire Dialect.

An American Specimen, humorous, by Mark Twain.

Little Feet, pathetic.

An Order for a Picture, a very acceptable pathetic selection, always popular.

How " Ruby " Played, a very humorous piece, giving a countryman's description of the playing of Rubenstein

Reply to Hayne, oratorical and good for teaching, by Daniel Webster.

The First Quarrel, dramatic and pathetic, by Tennyson.

Vashti, very popular, by Julia C. R. Dorr.

Her Letter, a story of early California, scene in Poverty Flat, by Bret Harte

Shoemaker's Best Selections No. 9

Compiled by Mrs. J. W. SHOEMAKER

Vice-President of The National School of Elocution and Oratory

200 pages. Cloth binding, 50 cents; Paper, 30 cents

The following are some of the most popular pieces in this number:

Mrs. Walker's Betsy, a story of humble life told in graphic language.

Bertha in the Lane, pleasing pathos, exemplifying a sister's sacrifice, by Mrs. Browning.

Mrs. Ward's Visit to the Prince, superior Yankee Dialect.

Selling the Farm, a pathetic story of farm life.

The White Squall, humorous, by William M. Thackeray.

Brier-Rose, a thrilling Norwegian story, very popular, by Hjalmar Hjorth Boyesen.

A Christmas Ballad, a pathetic Christmas story.

The National Ensign, a patriotic declamation.

Horatius at the Bridge, heroic, very popular, by T. B. Macaulay.

Lookout Mountain, German Dialect.

The Child on the Judgment Seat, moral and spiritual, good for Sunday-schools.

The Sailing of King Olaf, beautiful sentiment, excellent for vocal culture.

The Palace of the King, Scotch Dialect.

The Aged Stranger; or, I Was With Grant, humorous incident of the Civil War, by Bret Harte.

Baby's Visitor, encore.

Mine Vamily, German Dialect, by Charles Follen Adams.

The Ideal, encore.

Rover's Petition, good child's piece, by James T. Fields.

Pwize Spwing Poem, a dude's poem.

Potency of English Words, oratorical,

excellent literature, good for teaching, by John S. MacIntosh, D. D.

Thoughts for a New Year, for New Year's.

Master Johnny's Next-Door Neighbor, boy characterization, by Bret Harte.

William Goetz, humorous.

Connor, very pathetic and exceedingly popular.

The Song of the Camp, introduces the song of Annie Laurie, by Bayard Taylor.

Tribute to Washington, for Washington's Birthday.

St. George and the Dragon, dramatic.

The Yorkshire Cobbler, good for temperance occasions, Yorkshire Dialect.

Sam's Letter, and extract from Our American Cousin, a humorous impersonation of an English lord.

Unnoticed and Unhonored Heroes, oratorical.

School Begins To-day, appropriate for the opening of schools.

The Truth of Truths, excellent literature, good for teaching, by Ruskin.

Terpsichore in the Flat Creek Quarters, describes a dance among the Negroes, Darkey Dialect.

The Widow and Her Son, beautiful and pathetic, by Washington Irving.

Awfully Lovely Philosophy, characterization of a gushing æsthetic young girl.

Last Prayer of Mary, Queen of Scots, pathetic, the last hours of Queen Mary.

The First Party, humorous, child characterization.

Shoemaker's Best Selections No. 10

Compiled by Mrs. J. W. SHOEMAKER

Vice-President of The National School of Elocution and Oratory

200 Pages. Cloth binding, 50 cents; Paper, 30 cents

Special mention may be made of the following, which are some of the best pieces in this number:

Eulogy on Garfield, eulogistic of the life and death of President Garfield, by Hon. James G. Blaine.

The Phantom Ship, a tale of a slave ship, by Celia Thaxter.

Despair, dramatic, by Tennyson.

Washington Hawkins Dines With Col. Sellers, humorous, by Twain and Warner.

Drifting, a pleasing and always popular poem, by Thomas Buchanan Read.

The Law of Death, pathetic, by Edwin Arnold.

Tilghman's Ride, how he brought the news from Yorktown to Philadelphia.

A Frenchman on Macbeth, French characterization.

The Lost Found, pathetic, being an extract from Evangeline, by Henry W. Longfellow.

Dick Johnson's Picture, an interesting temperance story.

Theology in the Quarters, Negro Dialect.

The Death of Roland, heroic, the incident is that of a battle between the Christians and Saracens.

To the Survivors of the Battle of Bunker Hill, patriotic and oratorical, also good for teaching, by Daniel Webster.

The Shriving of Guinevere, a fine dramatic recitation, by Dr. S. Weir Mitchell.

A Reminiscence of Exhibition Day, humorous, by R. J. Burdette.

The Blind Lamb, a pleasing child's recitation, by Celia Thaxter.

The Old Year and the New, for New Year's, by Eben E. Rexford.

Little Rocket's Christmas, a pleasing Christmas story, by Vandyke Brown.

Larrie O'Dee, Irish Dialect.

The Schoolmaster Beaten, dramatic,

excellent for characterization. An extract from Nicholas Nickleby, by Charles Dickens.

Dot Baby off Mine, German Dialect, by Charles Follen Adams.

Caught in the Quicksand, dramatic, excellent piece for teaching, by Victor Hugo.

Nay, I'll Stay With the Lad, dramatic.

Little Dora's Soliloquy, child characterization.

Rev. Gabe Tucker's Remarks, Negro Dialect.

The Irrepressible Boy, introduces an inquisitive boy.

Herve Riel, a fine dramatic recitation by Robert Browning.

Jamie, dramatic and pathetic, very popular.

Armageddon, the war cry of the future by Edwin Arnold.

Tammy's Prize, Scotch Dialect.

New England's Chevy Chase, patriotic by Edward Everett Hale.

A Railway Matinee, very funny, excellent opportunities for various impersonations, by R. J. Burdette.

Mick Tandy's Revenge, pathetic, but with a pleasing ending.

The Sky, excellent literature, a beautiful description, good for teaching, by Ruskin.

Balaklava, a dramatic incident in the war of Russia.

Chickamauga, patriotic, good for Decoration Day.

The Wayside Inn, pathetic, by Adelaide A. Procter.

The True Story of Little Boy Blue, a pleasing child's piece.

Rizpah, the familiar Bible story in blank verse, dramatic and pathetic, parts to be sung

Shoemaker's Best Selections No. 11

Compiled by Mrs. J. W. SHOEMAKER

Vice-President of The National School of Elocution and Oratory

200 pages. Cloth binding, 50 cents ; Paper, 30 cents

This has always been one of the most popular numbers of the series. Among the many pleasing selections in this number may be mentioned the following :

Apostrophe to the Ocean, excellent for vocal training, by Byron.

An Arctic Aurora, an interesting description of the Northland.

The Bobolink, affords opportunities for the introduction of bird tones.

Catching the Colt, a good recitation for young folks.

The Child Martyr, an excellent child's piece.

The Clown's Baby, a pleasing incident of life in a mining camp.

The Convict's Soliloquy the Night Before Execution, exceedingly dramatic and pathetic.

Death of Little Dombey, pathetic, extract from Dombey and Son, by Charles Dickens.

The Dutchman's Snake, very amusing.

Echo and the Ferry, a beautiful description, good piece for impersonation, by Jean Ingelow.

Flash, the Fireman's Story, an amusing incident of a milkman's horse that had served its time in the fire department, by Will Carleton.

The Foxes' Tails ; or, Sandy Macdonald's Signal. This is one of the most deservingly popular humorous pieces in print, and is given with marked success by the best readers.

The Freckled-Faced Girl, humorous characterization of a pert young girl.

The Front Gate, humorous.

The Froward Duster, very amusing, by R. J. Burdette.

Garfield at the Wheel, patriotic.

The Grandmother's Apology, old lady characterization, by Tennyson.

Her Name, child characterization.

Jerry, introducing the impersonation of a newsboy, very popular

The Lisping Lover, encore.

Little Gottlieb's Christmas, a pleasing Christmas story of Germany.

Mice at Play, humorous, opportunities for a number of characterizations.

Modern Facilities for Evangelizing the World, oratorical, by Henry Ward Beecher.

Mona's Waters, highly dramatic.

The New Slate, child characterization.

Nicodemus Dodge, humorous, by Mark Twain.

No Kiss, encore.

The Old Year and the New, for New Year's, by Josephine Pollard.

One Flower for Nelly, pathetic Easter piece, by Rose Hartwick Thorpe.

The Prospects of the Republic, oratorical, by Edward Everett.

Queen Vashti's Lament, dramatic and pathetic.

Rock Me to Sleep, pathetic.

Romance of a Hammock, very clever humor.

The Shadow of Doom, dramatic recital, by Celia Thaxter.

Song of the Mystic, a beautiful moral and religious poem, by Father Ryan.

Sunday Fishin', Negro Dialect.

Supposed Speech of John Adams on the Declaration of Independence, patriotic, by Daniel Webster.

A Telephonic Conversation, humorous, by Mark Twain.

This Side and That, encore, by George MacDonald.

Thora, a Norwegian story, very popular, by Hjalmar Hjorth Boyesen.

Ticket o' Leave, dramatic, by George R. Sims.

Where's Annette ? dramatic.

The Wonders of Genealogy, humorous

Shoemaker's Best Selections No. 12

Compiled by Mrs. J. W. SHOEMAKER

Vice-President of The National School of Elocution and Oratory

200 Pages. Cloth binding, 50 cents ; Paper, 30 cents

Special mention may be made of the following superior selections:

Aunty Doleful's Visit, the incident is that of an old lady trying to cheer a sick niece by telling her all sorts of distressing news, by Mary Kyle Dallas.

Aux Italiens, an exceedingly popular selection, parts may be sung, by Robert Bulwer Lytton.

The Ballad of Cassandra Brown, a travestie on some of the modern forms of exaggerated elocution.

The Battle-Flag of Shenandoah, a patriotic poem pertaining to the Civil War, by Joaquin Miller.

The Bells, a superior selection for vocal culture, by Edgar A. Poe.

Bells Across the Snow, a pleasing Christmas poem, by Frances Ridley Havergal.

The Bishop's Visit, a good child's recitation, by Emily Huntingdon Nason.

The Blind Poet's Wife, a pleasing narrative and an excellent recitation, by Edwin Coller.

The Book Canvasser, humorous, by Max Adler.

A Brother's Tribute, a strong heroic and pathetic selection, good for G. A. R. occasions.

The Country School, humorous.

Earnest Views of Life, an instructive declamation, by Austin Phelps, D. D.

An Eastertide Deliverance, A. D. 430, good for Easter occasions.

The Engineer's Making Love, humorous, by Robert J. Burdette.

The Fall of Pemberton Mill, one of the most pathetic, dramatic, and generally effective recitations in print, contains singing parts, is exceedingly popular, by Elizabeth Stuart Phelps.

A Fly's Cogitations, a humorous description of a fly's meditations during its progress over the scalp of a bald-headed man.

Good-bye, a good encore piece, illustrating how women say good-bye to each other.

The Grace of Fidelity, a good Sunday-school selection.

How Girls Study, humorous, good opportunities for impersonation of different girl characters.

How the Gospel Came to Jim Oaks, pathetic, a story of a mining camp.

Interviewing Mrs. Pratt, an amusing experience of a reporter attempting to interview the wives of a Mormon.

Jesus, Lover of My Soul, a very pleasing selection, parts to be sung, by Eugene J. Hall.

Jimmy Brown's Steam Chair, very amusing.

Lasca, dramatic and pathetic, scene in Texas on a cattle ranch, exceedingly popular.

The Legend of the Beautiful, a strong spiritual piece, by Henry W. Longfellow.

Lincoln's Last Dream, a pathetic poem, good for recitation, by Hezekiah Butterworth.

The Maister an' the Bairns, Scotch Dialect.

Mine Schildhood, German Dialect, by Charles Follen Adams.

The Newsboy's Debt, a pathetic poem, by Helen Hunt Jackson.

Over the Orchard Fence, old farmer characterization.

Poor House Nan, pathetic, by Lucy H. Blinn.

Popular Science Catechism, humorous.

Receiving Calls, humorous ; extract from the diary of a minister's wife.

Santa Claus in the Mines, a popular Christmas story of a mining camp.

The Serenade, a good encore piece.

She Cut His Hair, humorous, by the Danbury News Man.

The Skeleton's Story, a fine dramatic description—prairie scene.

A Story of Chinese Love, a good encore piece.

Teddy McGuire and Paddy O'Flynn, Irish Dialect.

Temperance, a strong address on that subject by the Rt. Rev. John Ireland.

A Ter'ble 'Sperience, Negro Dialect, by Rev. Plato Johnson.

Total Annihilation, a good encore piece, sometimes known as "There aint goin' to be no core."

Shoemaker's Best Selections No. 13

Compiled by Mrs. J. W. SHOEMAKER

Vice-President of The National School of Elocution and Oratory
200 pages. Cloth binding, 50 cents; Paper, 30 cents

This issue has also been one of the popular numbers of the series. Among some of the good pieces which it contains are the following:

The Abbess's Story, a dramatic description, by Henry W. Longfellow.

After-Dinner Speech by a Frenchman, good French impersonation.

The Ancient Miner's Story, pathetic, by Will Carleton.

Aristarchus Studies Elocution, a travestie on some kinds of modern elocution.

At Last, a beautiful spiritual poem, by John G. Whittier.

Aunt Polly's George Washington, Negro Dialect.

Banford's Burglar Alarm, exceedingly amusing and very popular.

Canada, a pleasing tribute to our neighbors across the border.

The Chase, very dramatic, by Walter Scott.

A Child's Dream of a Star, very pathetic, by Charles Dickens.

The Chopper's Child, a good child's piece, by Alice Carey.

The Cloud, a beautiful description and a good teaching piece.

Ego et Echo, good encore piece, affording excellent opportunities for displaying the voice, by John G. Saxe.

The Humblest of the Earth Children, fine descriptive piece, good for teaching, by Ruskin.

In the Signal Box, a Station-master's Story, exceedingly pathetic but with a pleasing ending, by Geo. R. Sims.

Jehoshaphat's Deliverance, good for Sunday-schools.

The Little Quaker Sinner, a good girl's piece.

Lead the Way, a fine declamation, by Lyman Abbott.

The Legend of the Organ Builder, a pathetic description and a very popular piece, by Julia C. R. Dorr.

Let the Angels Ring the Bells, a pleasing Christmas poem.

Lord Dundreary in the Country, a very taking extract from "Our American Cousin," impersonation of an English lord.

Mary's Night Ride, an extract from "Dr. Sevier." It is an incident of the Civil War and is a very thrilling and dramatic selection; exceedingly popular, by George W. Cable.

Memorial Day, appropriate for Decoration Day.

A Methodist Class Meeting, humorous and pathetic, Yorkshire Dialect.

Mine Shildren, German Dialect, by Charles Follen Adams.

Mother and Poet, dramatic and pathetic, very popular, by Mrs. Browning.

A New Cure for Rheumatism, the treatment is the application of bees to the afflicted parts, very popular, by Robert J. Burdette.

The New Year, or Which Way, appropriate for New Year's, by Lyman Abbott.

The Old Continentals, a pleasing tribute to the soldiers of colonial times.

The Old Man Goes to Town, excellent opportunity for old-man characterization.

On the Stairway, encore.

Out to Old Aunt Mary's, one of the popular poems of the author, James Whitcomb Riley.

Our Relations to England, oratorical and a good teaching piece, by Edward Everett.

Regulus to the Carthagenians, familiar to all, but still a most acceptable declamation, by E. Kellogg.

A Rhymlet, encore.

Song of the American Eagle, a good patriotic poem.

The Spring Poet, humorous.

The Two Stammerers, the incident is that of two persons who claim to have been cured of stammering, but it is a question which is the worse stammerer of the two, very amusing and popular.

The V-a-s-e, illustration of the different pronunciations of the word in different localities, humorous and a good encore piece.

The Yosemite, a sublime description of the far-famed California Valley.

Shoemaker's Best Selections No. 14

Compiled by Mrs. J. W. SHOEMAKER

Vice-President of The National School of Elocution and Oratory

200 pages. Cloth binding, 50 cents; Paper, 30 cents

The following are among the popular selections in this number:

Ballad of the Wicked Nephew, a good humorous piece, by James T. Fields.

Battle of Morgarten, heroic, the incident is that of a battle between the Swiss and Austrians, by Mrs. Hemans.

Be a Woman, a beautiful and popular poem, by Dr. Edward Brooks, A. M.

Bill and Joe, a pleasing and clever humorous selection, by Oliver Wendell Holmes.

Brudder Yerkes's Sermon, Negro Dialect.

The Cow and the Bishop, a capital humorous selection containing excellent opportunities for impersonation.

A Culprit, humorous, by Margaret Vandegrift.

Daniel Gray, a beautiful description, by J. G. Holland.

The Day is Done, the ever-pleasing and popular poem, by Longfellow.

The Death of Steerforth, an exceedingly dramatic extract from David Copperfield, by Charles Dickens.

Destiny of America, oratorical.

Domestic Economy, humorous, by the Danbury News man.

The Drummer Boy of Mission Ridge, excellent for G. A. R. occasions.

The Finding of the Cross, a good missionary piece.

Going for the Cows, a description of country life, introducing various calls, by Eugene J. Hall.

The Great Issue, oratorical, good for teaching, by Edward Everett.

Jimmy Brown's Sister's Wedding, very funny.

June, the well-known poem, by James Russell Lowell.

Jupiter and Ten, encore, by James T. Fields.

King Harold's Speech to His Army Before the Battle of Hastings, heroic, by Bulwer Lytton.

The Lady Judith's Vision, a pleasing Christmas poem.

The Last Charge of Ney, oratorical.

The Life-Boat, pathetic, but with a pleasing ending, by Geo. R. Sims.

Military Supremacy Dangerous to Liberty, oratorical, good for teaching, by Henry Clay.

The Miseries of War, also oratorical and good for teaching, by Chalmers.

Money Musk, description of a negro dance, excellent opportunities for characterization, very popular.

A Mother's Portrait, a very pathetic poem, familiar but always acceptable, by Cowper.

Mr. Winkle Puts On Skates, humorous, by Charles Dickens.

Nearer Home, a beautiful spiritual poem. by Phœbe Cary.

The Night Watch, very dramatic, by Francois Coppee.

Pockets, a strong descriptive piece, by Julian Hawthorne.

The Puritan, a tribute to our forefathers, by George William Curtis.

The Romance of the Swan's Nest, a beautiful description, by Mrs. Browning.

A Second Trial, how a boy almost failed in his commencement oration, but was saved by his sister from doing so; very popular, by Sara Winter Kellogg.

The Ship of State, patriotic, an excellent declamation.

Sister Agatha's Ghost, humorous, Yorkshire Dialect.

The Soldiers' Home, Washington, for G. A. R. occasions, by Joaquin Miller.

The Sweetest Picture, a most acceptable pathetic poem. by Alice Cary.

A Tear of Repentance, a beautiful description, by Thomas Moore.

The Tender Heart, encore, by Helen Gray Cone.

Thoughts for the New Year, for New Year's.

Three Leaves from a Boy's Diary, humorous.

The Twenty-second of February, for Washington's Birthday, by William Cullen Bryant.

The Victor of Marengo, excellent declamation, good for teaching.

The Widow Cummiskey, clever Irish wit.

Ulysses, a pleasing description, good for teaching, by Tennyson.

Shoemaker's Best Selections No. 15

Compiled by Mrs. J. W. SHOEMAKER

Vice-President of The National School of Elocution and Oratory

200 Pages.   Cloth binding, 50 cents ;   Paper, 30 cents

For Recitals this is one of the best numbers in the series.   The following may be mentioned as among the popular pieces :

America, a patriotic poem.

The Bachelors, excellent humor.

The Bartholdi Statue, an eloquent tribute to the Goddess of Liberty, by Julian Hawthorne.

Beautiful Hands, pleasing sentiment.

Becalmed, very dramatic.

Childhood Scenes, a beautifnl description.

Christmas Guests, a good Christmas story.

The City of Is, a fanciful poem.

Commerce, a strong declamatory selection, good for teaching, by Edward Everett.

A Concord Love Song, encore.

David's Lament for Absalom, pathetic and popular, excellent for teaching, by N. P. Willis.

The Death of Jezebel, very dramatic.

Der Oak und der Vine, German Dialect, very popular, by Charles Follen Adams.

The Fading Leaf, a beautiful description, by Gail Hamilton.

Fall In ! 1860, an incident in the formation of the Southern Army ; an excellent piece for characterization, by George W. Cable.

Flag of the Rainbow, patriotic, by Thomas Dunn English.

The Golden Bridge, humorous

Grant's Place in History, an historical description.

The Gray Champion, a fine teaching piece, embodying the spirit of American freedom, by Nathaniel Hawthorne.

Guessing   Nationalities, humorous, good piece for characterization, by Mark Twain.

In the Children's Hospital, pathetic, by Tennyson.

Ireland to be Ruled by Irishmen, Irish patriotism, good for declamation, by William E. Gladstone.

Jem's Last Ride, pathetic.

King Arthur and Queen Guinevere, extract from "Guinevere" : a beautiful recitation, by Tennyson.

The Kiss Deferred, a pleasing pathetic poem, very popular.

La Tour d'Auvergne, heroic.

Little Christel, a child's piece.

Little Foxes, an instructive selection, by R. J. Burdette.

Little Maid with Lovers Twain, humorous.

Manhood, a stirring declamation, by George K. Morris, D. D.

Mr. Beecher and the Waifs, a pleasing incident that occurred in his own church.

Mrs. Picket's Missionary Box, good for missionary occasions.

Music in Camp, frequently known as "Music on the Rappahannock," parts to be sung, very popular.

An Old Roundsman's Story, for Christmas, by Margaret Eytinge.

Our Choir, encore.

Our First Experience with a Watch Dog, an extract from "Rudder Grange," very amusing and popular, by Frank R. Stockton.

A Perfectly, Awfully, Lovely Story, an aesthetic exaggeration.

The Price of a Drink, good for temperance occasions, by Josephine Pollard

She Wanted to Hear it Again, encore

Speech Against the Stamp Act, oratorical, and a good teaching piece, by James Otis.

A Song for the Conquered, a stirring patriotic poem.

A Story of an Apple, a good recitation for a boy, by Sydney Dyer.

A Strange Experience, a good girl's piece, by Josephine Pollard.

The Three Kings, a good descriptive poem, by Henry W. Longfellow.

A Tragedy on Past Participles, humorous.

The Two Runaways, Negro Dialect, humorous, very popular, by H. S. Edwards.

Watch Night, for New Year's, by Horatius Bonner.

The World We Live In, one of the author's characteristic graphic descriptions, by T. De Witt Talmage.

Shoemaker's Best Selections No. 16

Compiled by Mrs. J. W. SHOEMAKER
Vice-President of The National School of Elocution and Oratory
200 pages. Cloth binding, 50 cents ; Paper, 30 cents

This issue has always been one of the popular numbers of the series. Special mention may be made of the following excellent selections :

The Angel and the Shepherds, a description of the birth of Christ, being an extract from "Ben Hur"; can be accompanied with musical interludes, by Lew Wallace.

Back from the War, a graphic description ; good for G. A. R. occasions, by T. De Witt Talmage.

The Battle Hymn, oratorical and good for teaching.

Calls, a minister's somewhat curious boy endeavors to get an explanation of ministerial calls ; very funny.

The Chariot Race, a fine description and a strong dramatic selection ; one of the most popular pieces ever written, an extract from "Ben Hur," by Lew Wallace.

The Christening, an amusing incident of how a child was misnamed in the christening.

The Curse to Labor, a strong appeal for temperance among the laboring classes, by T. V. Powderly.

The Day of Judgment, an amusing incident of two children who thought the world had come to an end, by Elizabeth Stuart Phelps.

Decoration Day, a beautiful patriotic poem, by Wallace Bruce.

The Elf Child, sometimes known as 'The Gobble-uns'll Git You," by James Whitcomb Riley.

The First View of the Heavens, a beautiful description.

Fraudulent Party Outcries, oratorical and a good teaching piece, by Daniel Webster.

How the Celebrated Miltiades Peterkin Paul Got the Better of Santa Claus, a very amusing Christmas story.

An Invitation to the Zoological Gardens, a very funny stuttering piece.

The Jefful, affords good opportunities for baby talk and cries, by John Habberton.

Jimmy Hoy, a capital Irish Dialect prose selection, by Samuel Lover.

Lily Servoss's Ride, a fine dramatic selection. The incident takes place at the close of the War during the ravages of the Ku-Klux, by Judge Tourgee.

The Message of the Dove, a dramatic Easter poem, by E. Nesbit.

The Mourner a la Mode, a satirical poem on the mourning custom as observed in fashionable circles, by John G. Saxe.

The New South, a graphic description of the present condition of the South, by Henry W. Grady.

An Old Sweetheart of Mine, a very popular poem, by James Whitcomb Riley.

A Pin, clever humor, by Ella Wheeler Wilcox.

The Portrait, very dramatic and exceedingly popular, by Lord Lytton.

Praying for Shoes, pathetic, by Paul Hamilton Hayne.

Song of the Mountaineers, a patriotic poem, by T. Buchanan Read.

The Tell-Tale Heart, a murderer's confession, exceedingly dramatic, by Edgar Allen Poe.

That Waltz of Von Weber, a beautiful rhythmical poem, by Nora Perry.

The Thanksgiving in Boston Harbor, a splendid Thanksgiving piece, by Hezekiah Butterworth.

Topsey's First Lesson, an extract from "Uncle Tom's Cabin," very funny and affording excellent opportunities for characterization, by Harriet Beecher Stowe.

Toussaint L' Ouverture, oratorical, by Wendell Phillips.

The Two Pictures, the story of a beautiful child, who when grown to manhood was found in a felon's cell.

The Uncle, a man had murdered his brother and in attempting to tell the story to his nephew reveals his identity, intensely dramatic, by H. G. Bell.

Water and Rum, one of the author's most stirring appeals for temperance, by John B. Gough.

Wisdom Dearly Purchased, excellent declamation, by Edmund Burke.

Shoemaker's Best Selections No. 17

Compiled by Mrs. J. W. SHOEMAKER

Vice-President of The National School of Elocution and Oratory

200 Pages. Cloth binding, 50 cents; Paper, 30 cents

This is also one of the good numbers of the series, by some consid ered one of the best. Among the many good pieces may be mentioned the following:

Alexander's Feast; or, the Power of Music, a beautiful rhythmical poem, popular as a recitation and good for teaching, by Dryden.

Army of the Potomac, an excellent poem, for G. A. R. occasions, by Joaquin Miller.

The Army of the Potomac, a splendid prose selection, also good for G. A. R. occasions, by Chauncey M. Depew.

Aunt Melissy on Boys, Yankee Dialect, very amusing throughout, the particular incident being that of turkeys becoming intoxicated by eating corn soaked in rum, by J. T. Trowbridge.

Aunt Sylvia's First Lesson in Geography, Negro Dialect, an old Negro woman's first attempt at the study of geography.

Colloquial Powers of Dr. Franklin, a strong descriptive piece, good for teaching.

Dead on the Field of Honor, a good declamation.

Easter Morning, an Easter-tide oration, by Henry Ward Beecher.

The First Thanksgiving, a beautiful poem for Thanksgiving occasions, by Hezekiah Butterworth.

The Garfield Statue, an eloquent tribute to the martyred President, by Hon. Grover Cleveland.

The Heavenly Guest, a spiritual poem, translated from the Russian of Count Tolstoi, by Celia Thaxter.

How We Fought the Fire, an amusing poem, descriptive of a fire in a country village, by Will Carleton.

Inge, the Boy King, an excellent dramatic selection, Norwegian scene, by Hjalmar Hjorth Boyesen.

Jimmy Brown's Prompt Obedience, humorous.

Labor, a prose declamation, by Thomas Carlyle.

The Land of Thus and So, a fanciful poem, by James Whitcomb Riley.

The Legend of Rabbi Ben Levi, a beautiful and instructive poem, by Henry W. Longfellow.

Lexington, a patriotic poem pertaining to Revolutionary times, by Oliver Wendell Holmes.

The Little Match Girl, a pathetic Christmas story, by Hans Christian Andersen.

Lord Dundreary's Riddles, a popular extract from "Our American Cousin," impersonation of an English lord.

Lost, an excellent dramatic piece, good for temperance occasions, by L. M. Cunard.

Love of Country, patriotic and a good teaching piece, by Newton Booth.

The Low-Backed Car, very popular Irish Dialect poem, humorous, by Samuel Lover.

The Minuet, a pleasing poem, introducing the minuet step.

The Monk's Magnificat, a very popular poem in which a chant is effectively introduced, by E. Nesbit.

Mr. Brown Has His Hair Cut, a very amusing prose selection.

The Poor and the Rich, a fine moral and instructive poem, by James Russell Lowell.

The Ride of Collins Graves, a thrilling description of the bursting of a dam, by John Boyle O'Reilly.

Rome and Carthage, a strong dramatic declamation, by Victor Hugo.

The Rustic Bridal; or, the Blind Girl of Castle Cuille, a beautiful descriptive poem, affording opportunities for impersonations, by Henry W. Longfellow.

Sent Back by the Angels, pathetic and a very popular selection.

The Silver Plate, the incident is that of a child offering itself as a contribution to a missionary collection, by Margaret J. Preston.

Took Nodice, German Dialect.

The Usual Way, very clever humor.

The Vow of Washington, eulogistic of the work of Washington, by John G. Whittier.

What is a Minority? a fine oratorical selection, by John B. Gough.

A Wild Night at Sea, a strong dramatic description, by Charles Dickens.